JOANNE GREENBERG was born in Brooklyn, New York in 1932. She graduated from American University in Washington, D.C. and the University of London and she has also studied at Colorado University. In 1964 she published the highly-acclaimed *I Never Promised You a Rose Garden*, using the name "Hannah Green." Since then, under her own name, she has published three novels (THE KING'S PERSONS, THE MONDAY VOICES, and IN THIS SIGN—all available in Avon editions) and two collections of short stories (*Summering* and RITES OF PASSAGE).

Mrs. Greenberg lives in a mountain-top Colorado home with her husband and two teenage sons. In addition to her writing, she also teaches sign language and experimental elementary school classes in etymology, history, and structure of the English language.

Avon Books by Joanne Greenberg

THE KING'S PERSONS
IN THIS SIGN
THE MONDAY VOICES

RITES OF PASSAGE

JOANNE GREENBERG

BARD BOOKS / PUBLISHED BY AVON

Some of the stories in this volume have appeared earlier in The Denver Quarterly, The Transatlantic Review, McCall's Magazine, Redbook Magazine, Good Housekeeping, Hadassah Magazine and Works in Progress.

AVON BOOKS
A division of
The Hearst Corporation
959 Eighth Avenue
New York, New York 10019

First Bard Printing, August, 1973.

BARD TRADEMARK REG. U.S. PAT. OFF. AND
FOREIGN COUNTRIES, REGISTERED TRADEMARK—
MARCA REGISTRADA, HECHO EN CHICAGO, U.S.A.

Printed in the U.S.A.

To Judy Sue and Judith

CONTENTS

1   Rites of Passage

THE FARMER KEPT LOOKING AS people got off the train. One boy had jumped easily from the steps, but a girl had run up to him and they had gone off together.

The train was nearly empty now and the farmer looked at the people waiting to get down. Could it be the skinny runt who kept turning and looking for something to recognize? He was only a kid, that runt. Hobart Sanderson who had answered the ad had said he was sixteen. This kid was thirteen and not a day over, a pale kid with a kind of sudden way of moving; nervous, like a girl.

The farmer spat in the dust and began to walk from the parking line to the train. That runt, that was the kid all right—the liar! Schaller groaned to himself. The weather had been too dry, the truck was going to pieces, and now here was help for the summer—a scrawny runt with a putty face and girl's ways, a city-born smart aleck who wouldn't know a plough from a piss-pot!

The boy was poised on the top step looking over the heads of the people on the platform. It had been a

long ride and he was tired from staying still for so long.
. . . Where was Mr. Schaller?

The boy's heart began to pound with excitement and
fear; his hands were damp. He hadn't slept on the
train. He had spent the night peering into all the darkness that he owned. It was his first time away from
home. . . . What if Mr. Schaller didn't like him and
sent him back?

He tried to get away from the thought because it
made him dizzy, knowing how his aunts would nod
and cluck and fold their arms and keep him from the
freedom he needed. They would cluck away all his
hunger to be grown and a man. That hunger was already making them querulous and afraid.

Hobart wanted his boyhood behind him. It was a
boyhood through which he had gone without ever having fished, swung in a tree, walked in rain bareheaded,
sworn in blood, had a pet, or owned a penknife. His
life had been like the old house where he stayed with
his aunts, airless and overheated and fussily dusted,
yet always smelling of dust and old cloth.

He looked again over the small group of people
waiting. There was a man looking back at him; a
grizzled man, older than he expected, but standing
alone and very straight; a strong, old, bitter face.

Hobart fought back his hope and juggled his suitcase down the steps; then he went toward the man,
who had not moved. They faced each other and their
silence almost became a contest until the old man said,
"You Sanderson? Hobart Sanderson?"

Hobart had never been called by his last name
before. He forced himself to look straight at the old
farmer. "Yes, sir." Certain that the "sir" would please;
seeing it succeed only by the difference of a slight easing in the muscle of the man's cheek.

"All right, boy, let's get to the truck." And the
farmer sighed. He thought: He sure ain't much to look

at, but he seems eager enough. He did lie. Thirteen; not a day older. I wonder how come he wants a job like this so much?

He looked at the boy again, but this time there was sympathy as well as scorn. He'll soon see this ain't some rich man's push-button operation. He'll see the truck first and that'll begin it. What's the hours? he'll want to know. And how many other boys are there and how many automatic machines and how many nights off. . . ?

They came to the pickup. It was an old '41, bought third hand after the War when the new ones started coming out again and all the farmers along the river had to have a brand-new big Something to show how rich they were from feeding the soldiers.

As they stopped at the truck, the boy looked at the farmer for approval before swinging his suitcase into the back and getting in himself to sit beside his new employer. The seat was cracked and the cab smelled of age like wet feathers, but it was different from the age-smell of the aunts and their house. It was a male smell, like sweat and strength and natural anger; and the boy breathed the acrid air, glad that it wasn't lied away with lavender or cologne. His aunts always lied things away or denied them altogether. They un-heard dirty jokes and un-saw the Saturday-night drunks singing their way home; they un-smelled Time, rotting away the foundations of their house.

The farmer ground gears starting, swore, bucked backwards and stalled, restarted, turned out into the street, and soon they were riding west on the highway out of town, taking every bump with the tops of their heads to the roof of the cab.

There was a lot to see as they drove out toward the farm. From the edge of his eyes Schaller caught glimpses of the boy. He's looking at those Latchoga

River places—fat, river-land, picture-book farms. Look your fill; it ain't where *you'll* stay.

Finally, with an almost fierce delight, he rammed the truck left so that it shuddered and squealed onto the unpaved road that led away from the green farms and lushly shaded white houses and into the rock-thrust uplands where the soil was poorer and the living harder to pull from it. Elemental. The boy sighed with pleasure, but the farmer heard disappointment in it and was, for a moment, maliciously happy. "I didn't tell you this was gonna be no baby-game. I don't work my hired men no harder than I work myself."

The boy said, "I'll do my best, sir," but his tone wasn't resigned or sour, and the farmer wondered if he was talking to a half-wit. Then he remembered having said "men." Hired men. Maybe that was what had done it. It was easy to see the kid was scrawny. Maybe it was what he wanted to hear, that he was thought of as a man. It could be a smart thing to do— praise him a little and then bait him along so he'd work harder to prove himself. The thought gave Schaller a brief ease from the secret pain that assaulted him everywhere. Let the rich Latchoga farmers wonder about all the work he could get out of one stringy kid for keep and two dollars a day.

They went up, leading their dust-cloud past where the farms began to spread wide apart. Wild hedges and high weeds lined the road but only where the runoff water could come to feed them.

They passed an opening in the hedges and the farmer said, "This here's Koven's place." He said it so that the boy immediately knew what his feelings were for this Koven. "Hold on, boy, here comes the rut!"

The truck hit it straight on; the leaf springs screamed, the frame shuddered, and a terrible rattling seemed to disengage each part from every other and hold it for a second, separate and suspended, until hurling everything down to clash together with a misfitting grind. Schaller swore and they rode on. He read the boy asking in his mind why he hadn't slowed down for the rut. Might as well tell him; he'd learn soon enough. "He put that rut there—Koven."

Hobart hadn't been thinking about the rut or the truck, but now he looked up, incredulous at what the farmer was saying. "But why—?"

"Put it there for spite. He's always spited me, Koven. Town is back there, so he never comes this far on the road. Me, I have to come past his house to get to my place. When he hears me comin', he sneaks behind that hedge-fence of his and watches me ridin' along in this old truck. I'll have to slow down, he figgers—slow and be humbled, and listen to him laughin'. Nossir, I don't bend for nobody. A *man,* a man don't snivel. He holds his peace."

They turned into a hole in the hedge and the boy saw the house. It had a gape-window, abandoned look to it. Going through the tangle that bordered the road it seemed as though the house was hiding behind it. The boy had a momentary feeling of fear, but he put it to his newness.

The front of the house was weed-grown, and when the truck stopped and Hobart got out, he got his socks full of burrs. He took his suitcase down and Schaller led him in to change his clothes in a sour-smelling, unused room off the kitchen. A succession of hired men had lain on the mattress of its sagging bed and had bad dreams.

When Schaller came in later with a blanket and smelled the room and all the years of hired men, drunk and sober, he hauled the mattress outside to freshen. "I'm gonna kersene this for bedbugs," he said, and when he saw the boy watching: "Don't stand there— get busy. The sickle is up at the barn. Go sickle off them patches around the trees back of the house."

The tangle of weeds choking the few fruit trees was too high for a mower, and the land was too rocky and uneven for anything but hand-sickling. All through the hot afternoon the boy worked, beating against the weeds with his curved weapon. By the middle of the afternoon his legs were weak and the muscles at the back of his thighs and knees were quivering with exhaustion. The sun blinded him in a white-hot glare while he worked, and only as the afternoon tipped downward did he understand that the sickle, although it was very sharp, was a tool, not a machine. It was powered only by his arm.

He had to watch out for stones on which the steel sparked. Sometimes the edge of a stone would turn the sweep of his wicked edge up and only by a hairbreadth would he miss being cut. He knew that if he got too tired, he wouldn't be able to move out of his own way fast enough. He came nearer and nearer to cutting himself. What he needed was not strength, but fury. He thought that if he sorted among his hatreds for something to attack, he could swing with the anger he needed to break the thousand delicate straw stalks an inch above the ground.

Schaller came with water at about five. "Quit around here for today. I got to show you where things are while it's still light. Hey, boy——" He was looking at the hand still gripping in its spasm of exhaustion around the handle of the sickle. The knuckles were covered with blood. "You been cuttin' too close. Rocks'll cut you to bone if you ain't careful, an' even the weeds you cut on the stroke before can hurt you bad."

"I'm all right," the boy said, and pried the sickle from his right hand. "It doesn't really feel sore."

"What's your first name, anyway—I can't keep callin' you Sanderson."

"Hobart, sir, but they call me Hobe."

It was a lie. No one had ever called him anything

but Hobart, and sneeringly, in school, for the things which had been done to him and which he had done to himself.

"Okay, Hobe, you ain't sore now, but you're gonna be plenty sore tomorrow. You quit over here like I said."

The boy was proud of himself to have to be stopped.

They walked back over the field together, Schaller talking now and then and pointing out different details as they went. Their shadows went before them, drawn tall by the westering light. The boy was trying with all he had to keep his mind on what the farmer was saying, but he was losing a battle with sleep. As he walked, he wondered dreamingly how long it had been since he had drawn a shadow beside a man, and how long it would be, if ever, before his shadow would be the shadow cast by a man.

After a tour of the barn they went to the house to make supper. Hobart picked up the mattress and, stumbling with exhaustion, carried it to the airless room off the kitchen where he let it fall on the bed. He fell on top of it and drowned immediately in a steamy sleep.

Schaller hadn't realized it, but he had been looking forward to supper with the boy. He hadn't had a hot meal in so long that his thought of the boy's being there set hunger-water running in his mouth. It wasn't worth while firing up the cookstove for just one. He made coffee for himself every morning on a little hot plate, but the rest of the day he would drink it cold with beans or spaghetti out of the can. He got so that he didn't even sit down to eat. With the boy there would be meals.

He lit a cigarette and went into the dusty front room. . . . It was having nobody to eat with that bothered him so much that he ate his cold food as quick as he could get it down. He wasn't lonely working around the farm all day, but at night—that was poverty —to work all day and walk home to an empty house where no woman stood wreathed in cooking steam, waiting to put his hot supper on the table and ask him about his day.

The world is a liar's place, he thought, but at least nobody knew how bitter it had been for him, because he never let on how much he knew about people's lies to him and their laughter. How easing it would be to have someone who knew, who shared—maybe even someone who could watch part of the night while he lay at peace and slept—someone as patient and silent as he, patient enough to wait while the mice—squeaking, scratching, silent thieves—gathered in the shadow of safe holes and began to come out. He knew that while he slept, soft-bodied, furry thieves were teasing him from the shadows, running across the floor, snatching, running back to twitch whiskers in amusement for the avid family mouths and the laughter of complacent safety.

And that was Koven. Koven was all the friendly greetings and offers of help and all the secret scrabbling that crept to steal everything Schaller had. Koven and his friends snatched apples and peaches off Schaller's trees and plums off his special bushes. They spooked his chickens and dried up his cows, and in town they'd meet him at the hardware store or at the bank and greet him like beady-eyed mice, all whisker-twitch and eager and full of comfort.

"That's a difficult acreage, you got there," they'd say, handing over their piles of money into the teller's prison and humbling themselves with oily ease. "Tell you plain, it's gonna be a scratch to get the boy paid to college next year. . . ."

Schaller laughed. Some watchman, the runt! He didn't even have the strength to eat his supper.

The farmer got up and went through the kitchen, noticing it objectively for the first time, as if through the kids' eyes. It had all the outward things that were shown in pictures of warm, happy old homesteads: the old table and the big wood stove. They were things he had grown up with. Now there were tears of grease weeping down the walls behind that stove, bits of bark and wood on the floor in little piled islands where they had been kicked or blown. And from the pantry, the closet, the cupboards where his mother's preserving things still stood, there were sounds—the sounds of the Intruders, their funny running to print the dust of the shelves where he could not help but see it—mouse and cockroach generations eating, fighting, bearing, and dying in the darkness of his pantry; disappearing less quickly and less fearfully every time he opened the pantry door and cut the darkness.

When the boy woke, the farmer was standing over his bed with a cup of boiled coffee. "Sit up, boy—it's day."

But it was dark, dark as the boy's confusion. When he tried to move in his bunched, sleep-damp clothes, a grinding ache moved out to grip the muscles of his back, legs, and shoulders. It was so sharp it made him shiver. He reached for the cup that was held out to him, grateful to the farmer but confused by the long sleep and frightened of the awful pains that warped along his arm so that he could barely lift it.

"Come on," Schaller said. "It's past five." He looked at the boy carefully. "You sore, ain't you. You too sore to work today." He said in a knowing tone as if he had expected the disappointment all along.

"No," the boy said, "no sir." He gritted his teeth and pulled himself up, all the cords in his body straining as though they would tear.

The coffee was bitter but clearing. When he finally

stood up, carrying all the crying fibers, pulling against the pull of simply standing, he realized that he hadn't even taken off his shoes. Thank God. He wouldn't have to bend for another few moments.

They went out together in the dew-wet gray darkness. They weeded the vegetable patch and cultivated around the potatoes and set stone on two retaining walls where runoff had carried the topsoil away with it.

By early afternoon, the boy's body had endured all it could. It rebelled. He dropped a stone. When he bent to pick it up, he fumbled, dropped it again on his foot, stood up, blind with pain but unable to bend again or lift the stone off his foot. In color-pocked dark pictures, he saw his aunts, two wild and gesticulating witches. He would never be a man. He would always fail.

Schaller saw the boy standing in a dumb anguish, and he came over, muttering about hired help that had no stay. Then he stopped and stared at the boy. Tears were running down his face; there was a rock crushing his foot and he was just standing there. "Hey, Hobe!" Schaller bent down and pushed the rock away and saw, as he bent, the boy's blistered hands hanging limp at his sides. "Hobe"—the boy made a faint sound—"what did you do that for?"

Hobart mumbled something, still seeing pictures of himself in his days of shame and failure. There was one he remembered when the boys chased him down the hill from school, screaming as if they were curses, words he had said: *"Puce, mauve, la di-da!"* Over and over.

Mauve. . . . He was despised not for ignorance, but for the degrading things he knew, for never having learned which parts of his knowledge were degrading—which parts he must never admit to. He could tell faille from crepe, and he knew this was forbidden. He was

familiar with all the embroidery stitches, because his
aunts discussed them at length; he could tell Alençon
from Chantilly lace, a peplum from a fichu. All that
and much more was forbidden; but the colors he knew
had deceived him. Boys are not supposed to know
puce or mauve or cerise or cerulean; they mustn't
know the names of flowers, although trees are all right.
Damn the mauve! If only he could recant and say
purple and let them flog him and forgive him. . . .

"Sit down—you look like you was goin' to pass out."

He half fell to the rocky ground. Schaller hunkered
down beside him. The kid was a puny runt, but he
was trying. Look at those hands.

"I guess I got too tired," Hobe said. "Please give me
another chance, sir. I'll be all right and it won't take
me long to build myself up."

Schaller let him worry for a while. They were sitting
facing the northwest boundary of the farm. There the
hill swelled itself slightly, leveled and rose again. The
level place separated Schaller's land from Koven's. A
person couldn't see Koven's house or barn from here,
but where the hill leveled he could see the creek between
the two farms. Schaller had depended a lot on the
fish that used to be in that creek. Koven had fished
it too, but he didn't need the fish. Now they were
gone. Wastes from upstream, Koven said. Maybe so;
maybe Koven, who said he didn't like to lie, had
gotten someone to walk upstream and put the poison
in to flow down past the farms and take Schaller's
food away from him.

The boy was looking at him, begging to be kept on.
Schaller began to be a little sorry for him. Hobe wasn't
stupid. A boy could make a sight more money collect-
ing scrap or doing yard work, and yet here he was
working his heart out, trying to make good. Schaller
scorned the vulnerable things in Hobe that made him
work, but he also felt a sympathy which was strange

for him. His mind seemed to be going two ways: turning back and forth as it had once turned back and forth at the sight of Koven, prosperous in the new pickup he had gotten by feeding the soldiers who killed for him and were killed. When others got the news, Schaller had to settle for the castoff. He had always had a pride in himself, but soon he had realized how people were laughing at him, scorn behind smiles as they passed him on the street. He had watched and waited and kept his peace, and then he had begun to notice the little things that they were doing to get at him. Always in the background, with his pursed lips and words of comfort so quickly—Koven. Bearing all of these things had become his life.

"You see that stream up there?" and the boy turned his head toward where the finger pointed. "There used to be fish in there, before he poisoned 'em, Koven." It was the first time he had said it to anyone else. The boy turned to look at him in wonder. The words were hanging in the air before Schaller's face, said, part of the world now, and real as the rocks where they were sitting.

The boy struggled up, still pale, but sure that everything was all right. He was going to be kept on. What tact real men have—to say things without long speeches and selfish calls for gratitude or guilt! "He poisoned 'em on purpose?" Hobe said, and his voice split embarrassingly so that both of them winced a little.

Schaller turned into the sun and faced the boy, his eyes squinting in the light. His intensity was so great that every muscle and sinew seemed to be drawn fine in him; his voice hummed with it. "On purpose. He'd like to see me fail here—give up and die. It 'ud mean the whole hill for him, and knowin' what I know about how he got his money—he don't like it that I'm here."

He stopped abruptly. It was enough. Koven's hate might interest Hobe, but it wouldn't do to scare him

—to show him how brave the mice, the enemies, were becoming in all the bins and corners, and in the walls of his house. He stopped himself and looked at the boy who was standing up, swaying. There was a look of bafflement on Hobe's face. Well, it was good for him to be puzzled a little. Schaller thought about those raw-rubbed hands and didn't know whether he should laugh or pity the boy trying so hard to have a man's pride.

"If you wanna fix them hands," he said, "I'll tell you how to do it. You piss on 'em. Hurts at first, but it takes the softness out of 'em an' helps you raise a callus quicker." Then he turned away. "I'm goin to the barn. Then we'll eat."

As he walked away, he heard the sound of the boy urinating, and a gasp, bitten off, as the acid ran over the raw flesh of his palms and fingers. It was the old way, the way he'd learned himself. No doubt there were a dozen kinds of creams and salves nowadays that you could get in the drugstore for two dollars. Everybody was too rich for plain piss any more. He went on into the barn.

They established habits and ways with each other. The boy was quick and willing. After a succession of half-wits or boys from the school where the State was training them to be half-wits, this boy seemed like a regular genius. It irked Schaller, when he thought about it, how the State quit letting him have those feebleminded boys for the summer. Coming back with bad habits. . . . What the hell did they know—a bunch of damn soft social workers, smooth-handed city——.

There were times when he would stand in the dim barn, besieged from all sides, worried and hounded by his enemies, each too small to see or too quick to catch. They wanted his land and his dreams. They had made his hopes fade to failure and they had begun to lie to him in his failure and then to laugh at him. Laughter has to grow or stop. It grew to scorn, burning him and destroying his land. Gradually, secretly it grew, mouths going behind hands, faces turning away as much as they dared. There was no safety outside the shrinking limits of his farm. The rest of the world was armed with poison and laughter and was waiting for him. If it happened that Hobe came in and saw Schaller standing in the barn with his secret suffering, he would pretend he didn't notice, going about his work like a sacristan when there was someone praying in the church.

They finished clearing the trees and diking the hill near the line. They planted, weeded, fixed fences, improved the chicken run and the faulty brooder, harvested rocks and stones in endless abundance to be piled at the sides of fields and ditches. Hobe was toughening perceptibly. The calluses on his hands, of which he was inordinately proud, were thick and scarred. His body, while still stringy, had taken on a whiplike resilience, and his carriage was straight and dignified, more like the old man's. He was beginning to comb his hair like the old man too, straight forward from the back of the head and kept short with a straight razor.

Hobe went to his room one evening to get his towel before washing up at the pump. It was mid-July and the windowless place had been sweltering and damp so that he sweated heavily when he slept and lay in his bed as if in a swamp of his own juices. When he walked into the room, he saw it was empty. The mattress was gone, the suitcase that had been under the bed, his other pants that hung on a nail, the night-mug he could never bring himself to use, the water glass he kept by the bed—all of it was gone. He turned and heard Schaller coming in to get ready for supper. "Mr.——"

"Oh?" And Schaller dropped a match into the wood stove and saw it catch to the papers and kindling, "I guess you're wondering where your stuff is. . . ." Then he turned back to the stove, fussing with the coffeepot and getting the grease hot to fry with. The boy was held with a wild fear that struggled and questioned itself for what he had done.

For Schaller, moving the stove-plate and putting in larger pieces of wood, it was a new experience, this knowledge he had of what someone else was thinking. Never before had he been able to read minds when they were not thinking about him. When Koven was thinking, Schaller could hear in his head, the clear words of Koven's thoughts, even while the hypocrite was offering sympathy or when he passed by in town with his mind seeming to be on other thoughts. The kid's fear had no words, but it was there all the same and easy to figure. He didn't want to torment Hobe, but somehow he found himself playing the boy like a fish. He couldn't say right then what he had done with Hobe's things, and Hobe couldn't come straight out and ask him, so they played taut-line, slack-line while the dinner cooked.

Schaller was beginning to feel a kind of admiration for that kid. A month ago when he had come, there would have been none of this pride or bravery in him, nothing that could stand looking at the possibility of ruin and endure in silence. Schaller was suddenly moved by what Hobe had become. He had become proud and strong by imitation. The pride and strength in Hobe were Schaller's own—it was like what a father would do. He was glad, even though it had taken time to get all the things out of that room while Hobe was working over by the boundary. Still, for some reason, he couldn't release the boy from his worry. It had become a test for Hobe and then for both of them.

They sat down and ate. They had fried meat and

beans and fried potatoes and today, canned peaches for dessert. Schaller sold the small supply of butter and milk he got so they had coffee and canned milk and they covered their bread thickly with mayonnaise and peanut butter. The peanut butter had been Hobe's idea.

The boy looked at Schaller, at his straightness. It hurt him that he was afraid to ask. If he'd done anything wrong, Schaller would have told him right then. It was the way men were, direct and sure. Finally The Man got up and said, "Take that other table-chair and put it upstairs in the room down the hall on the right. We got no use for it down here, and it just gets in the way. You go do that now. I got something I want to see to outside."

Hobe struggled up the narrow stairs with the chair. He realized that he had never been upstairs where Schaller slept, and that he had never even been curious about it, as if it was something beyond him. Schaller's sending him up meant that he was being let in to a more personal part of the house, and as he worked the chair up, trying to keep its legs away from the stairs, he began to be curious about the rooms. He had to tell himself that he would do his errand without looking into any other room but the one to which he was being sent. He could have saved himself the trouble. All the doors on the left side were closed. He turned to the right and saw a door open.

His things were there. The two windows were opened for the breeze. His bed, neatly made, was standing so that he could look out over the roof to where the road was, screened from the house by the brush. A big old maple stood outside the windows, making cool green sounds in the light wind. His suitcase had been put up on the closet shelf, his clothes hung on hooks in the closet. It had all been done with great care and forethought. It was wonderful—it was a sign from Schaller that Hobe was more than just a summer boy; it was like being born and raised here, not with the weakening, worrying old-maid aunts. He heard Schaller coming in below. "Hey, boy, you still up there?"

"Coming right down, sir!" he shouted, and then stood confounded. How was he going to thank Schaller? Too little would make it seem as if he didn't appreciate what the farmer had done for him—too much would ruin the gift. His aunts always ruined things by talk-talking them to death. Men were silent because they understood, because their understanding went deeper than the need for words. Schaller was moving around downstairs and Hobe left his new room quickly, closing the door after him. When he returned to the kitchen, he saw that Schaller's face hadn't changed. He wasn't smiling or waiting for thanks. He knew; his boy knew. That was enough. Hobe's gratitude was as deep for the silence as for the move and the way it had been done. He forgot the tormented dinner he had choked down and the power of his fear that he might somehow offend or displease the man who was Man to him. Neither of them ever spoke about the change.

It wasn't until he was in bed that Hobe remembered his knife. He had been lying quietly, dawdling on the bridge between rest and sleep. The scenery of his thoughts was spread out below him in rich and varied patterns. He looked down from his height, wishing to select a last thought slowly. He could be a prince, beloved by his father's people, but feared too, because of his silent power. The power would be . . . He thought very suddenly about the knife and he was shocked back full awake, trembling. The knife. Schaller had taken his bedding and moved it. He must have found the knife that Hobe kept hidden under his mattress. Why had he kept it? Hobe had forgotten the knife was there but Schaller had seen it and now he knew all of Hobe's bad thoughts, the ugly thoughts

he had about his aunts and their home and the shame
he had there. Schaller could go into his mind, and
God, the shame that would be exposed there for his
scorn! Hobe had managed to keep the knife hidden
from his aunts. It was his secret; a violent and male
thing in that rotting house of old women. He had not
been able to hide it from a real man. Somehow the
knife would suggest the elaborate night fantasies he had
of using it, stabbing people, hurting them, letting out
blood, purging them and himself. Sometimes he had
dreams of being imprisoned and of having to stab and
slash himself free. Schaller would despise him.

He got up, stumbling in the dark of the unfamiliar
new room. His body seemed to blur into the blurred
panic of his mind and he bumped his shin and stubbed
his toe, stupid with the resignation of being found out.
He moved dumbly, feeling for his suitcase in the dark
of the closet, and then pushing it too hard so that he
brought it down with a glancing blow on his head.
His eyes filled with tears. God! And The Man was right
across the hall, maybe knowing by the noises what
he was trying to do. He searched in the suitcase, in
the drawer of the washstand near his bed. There was
a mouse in the drawer. Its feet scratched in terror, and
it squealed, trying to get away from him. His hand
brushed against its nest—something soft, and scraps of
paper torn up. He shut the drawer and it shut loud
with his shock. He began to tremble. He had to get
back into bed, and as he did, his hand went under the
mattress by habit, or out of a hope he didn't even feel
in a conscious way. It touched the knife without recognition, moved up, caught to something in his mind,
moved back, touched the knife again, gripped it, took
it out and then went over it in the dark again and
again to make utterly and absolutely sure that it was
the knife, his knife. He lay holding it, comforted,
thinking about Schaller.

After the first relief, he realized that Schaller couldn't have missed seeing it. When he took up the mattress, he must have seen the knife, and then, in honor, closed his mind to the secret thing, as he closed his mouth on his own pain, keeping it private; in a way, sacred. He could almost hear Schaller's mind-voice saying: Boy wants a knife, that's his business. He had put it back where it belonged. He had understood.

As Hobe's fear thinned, he stretched against the coolness of clean sheets, wanting his sleep now. Outside, the purple-black mass of the maple tree moved slowly with the night wind. Its leaves lifted cool air to him. He began to leave wakefulness, holding to it only by a very slender strand of thought. He wondered why his aunts had consented to let him come at all. They always fussed about dirt and danger, following behind any fun or adventure with dustpans, and mouths set. Dust. Hands like dried leaves. And he was a duty, a loudness in their afternoon silences, dirty shoes in their vestibule. They didn't really want him there. They were all dust, dry . . . He let the thread fall and slept.

In the morning when he was washing up, he remembered about the mouse in the washstand drawer. He didn't want to kill anything while he himself was safe and happy. If he hadn't been looking for the knife, he might never have opened the drawer at all. The mouse wasn't hurting anything. He would let her and her children live—besides he was too busy to fuss with mice. He and Mr. Schaller would be picking tomatoes all day today. . . . He tucked his shirt in and hurried downstairs.

Schaller liked Hobe working beside him. With Hobe there it was a farm. Sometimes he could hear people thinking things about his place when they rode by. They thought: Old Schaller's place—he lets it run down.

Schaller is too old to keep up a farm. But Hobe made him feel angry again, rather than despair when he heard those voices. Koven was still pushing the stones for his retaining wall over the lip of the ditch, still scheming to take all the water, still spooking the cows, but Hobe made him feel vigorous and strong enough to want to fight Koven's plans again. His hate was clean, as it had been once, not sickened and weakened with an old man's helplessness.

They bent over the rows of tomatoes rhythmically. A man gives up a lot to stand straight. Bent over, the sun warms all along his back; it loosens his muscles and eases his bones. But a man who has been laughed at, put to shame—he's got to give up the comforts, he's got to harden and be straight. All right, Koven— spy all you want with your damn spyglass. You never see me anything but straight when I stand. I'm hard now, hard as something that's been tempered for fifty years. There will be a day, Koven, and the world will know it. . . .

When Schaller came to himself, he found that he had pulled ten of the tomatoes off the vine instead of twisting them. The boy hadn't seen. He would cut around the telltale hole and say they were for eating later. "I got us some nice tomatoes here," he said, and took them to the house quickly so the boy wouldn't see them.

The kitchen window looked over the tomato patch where the boy moved, bending steadily, not wasting a motion. Schaller knew that he himself and his embattled farm had done that for the boy. What do you say now, you soft, city social workers? Last month, a half hour of that kind of bending and Hobe would have fainted dead away.

Schaller began to cut the mangled ends from the tomatoes where he had torn them, and with the knife in his hand, he thought about how sharp it was. It was sharp enough to slice through a tomato and into a man's hand, and so quick that it would be done before there was time to think about it. Koven could die. Snap your fingers—he could die that quick.

When Schaller looked out the window at the boy again, he seemed to see him changed, in a changed landscape by a changed light. Hobe had come to him eager and puny, a kid so scared he had a knife in bed to fight off ghosts. Now he was strong and steady, that boy. He had worked and been hurt on this starving land, known hot sun and hard rain, worked dawn till dark. Dear God, it wouldn't matter; none of it would count for anything while Koven was draining all the plenty away. Schaller looked again and he seemed to see Hobe bowed like a beaten slave in the field. He was pulling exhaustion from the earth, harvesting agony. It wouldn't matter that he was patient and enduring—it was all for nothing. The harvest would be poor; the prices kept low again by Koven and his men to bring the farm to ruins. There was nothing for him and the boy but to be laughed at, beaten, and laughed at again. No profit, no wages. The boy was going to be broken in his first moment of being a man. Why doesn't anyone help him get even? Why doesn't anyone help him be a man?! Schaller found his eyes filling with tears. He couldn't remember when this had happened except when he was out in the wind or the cold. For a moment he was confused about the tears. In their blurring, he cut his finger.

When the farmer came to the tomato patch, Hobe was a little slow to straighten. It was disappointing to have Schaller come back before the row was finished. Bending didn't bother his back any more, but he had a habit of slouching and he had to pull himself up to match the straightness of The Man. He felt and then he saw the terrible sadness in Schaller. Other men broke in the middle when they were suffering. They bent from the shoulders. Hobe had seen it in movies dozens of times. Men who took their suffering standing straight—they were the heroes; they bettered everything they touched. Sorrow was richer for passing through them; pain had dignity because they lived it. Schaller only said what any hero would say—"Let's finish this row and then go in and get some lunch."

For the first time in his life, Hobe was not satisfied with reticence. He ventured from it timidly. "Is something the matter, sir?" Schaller only looked to where the boy had stopped and gauged his place with his eye and said, "Come on, son, let's finish the row."

He had said "son." The word made Hobe dizzy. He bent at his place and began picking again, muttering to himself against his hope. Schaller was troubled . . . had things on his mind . . . was thinking of someone else . . . hadn't meant it. But later, sorting and packing the boxes ready for town, Schaller used the word again.

Hobe lay in bed, forcing himself to stay awake. The night was vibrant with moonlight and the fall of the dew. When the time was right, he would know it and he would get up and creep out to the north hill where he could stand under the open sky for his ceremony. Maybe it seemed a little like what a kid would do, making a regular rite out of it, but even men had ways of breaking the walls of their pride, exploding from silence every once in a while. You saw them in the bars, yelling—even crying sometimes. They had ceremonies too. The drag drivers drove through his town at night; he could remember hearing them, their speed crying against the brakes. Every Saturday night they would insult the tyranny of sleepers in ceremonies of power and danger. Hobe couldn't have speed or whiskey or brawls. He wasn't even sure he had the strength to keep his own promise.

When it was time, he got up and opened his door. He was afraid of the awful silence of the house. He drifted through it, trying to think of himself as smoke moving across water. In the middle of the hall he stopped. It would look ridiculous, him standing in the moonlight in his underwear. He tiptoed back and got his pants. He would carry them outside and put them on there.

As he left again, turning down the hall, his belt buckle banged against the doorframe. He had to wait while the sound rang and rang, and he listened for the noises of Schaller turning in his sleep, waking up, wondering, getting up, coming to see, finding him; finally getting the truth because Hobe couldn't lie. . . . He forced himself away from thinking about it and listened again. There was nothing. The silence had closed over his mistake. He went on down the hall and felt out the voice of each board and then each step of the stairs, slowly. Then to the door. A board cried with his weight. He stopped. Then he opened the door and he was out in the night, down from the porch and wading in the dew that was cold on his bare feet.

He looked up at the sky and over the farm that was familiar to him only in daylight. Everything he saw responded to his ceremony; it was all ordered and planned in a processional rhythm: the system of stars and planets, the seasons of this farm and the precedence of its chores, the rise of the hills and the gathering of the dew. Yet as he looked at it all—earth, sky, stars, dew—it all seemed a wild, joyful profusion of things spilling over the rims of the world and the borders of heaven. All at once, gravity couldn't hold him prisoner. He broke into a run, stopped, capered, and sprang. The incredible plenty of everything took hold of him and when it came to him that this same fullness was in him, his body and his mind, he could barely keep from crying aloud with joy, singing and shouting as he ran. He was strong; he could run the hill and his wind wouldn't fail him. He was tough and fleet and happy. More than that, better than that, he had forever ahead of him to know this wild, over-flowing joy. He ran headlong up the hill, tripping over ruts and stones, falling sometimes, scrambling up to run again.

When he got to the top of the hill, he was tired, but only because he didn't feel like running down again. He had come to do an important thing, a thing that would seal his life forever in man's image. He put on his pants, listening to the night sounds. He found himself glad for the warmth of his pants. He was glad for everything. He felt for the first time in his life that he was being what he was meant to be, and so growing, coming into his season like the things of this land that he was beginning to know. For a moment he stood and enjoyed the tremendous vanity of his belated self-awakening. Hadn't he made all this his by his own work? Hadn't he come into all of this because of the depth of his feeling? Only such feelings could give a person title to the land and to The Man. It was why he had come to the hill tonight.

The moon had begun low. Night-riding clouds had tried to extinguish it, but it had ridden clear and was up high over his head now. He would have to get on with his ceremony and back to bed. It would be child-ish and stupid if he swore allegiance in ceremonial words tonight and fell asleep over the chores tomor-row. He spoke aloud, formally, as well as he could. Some of it was what he remembered from movies or books. He wanted something ancestral and eternal to say. "I, Hobart Sanderson, being of sound mind and body, I'm going to swear something and it's going to stand. Forever. Mr. Schaller called me son. And I swear that. I swear to be his son and to think about him like he was my father and defend him against all enemies foreign and domestic, and all danger, and never to have bad thoughts that would make him be sorry I was his son, and to keep faith with him forever. And I'm going to seal it."

Oh, hell! He had forgotten to bring his knife. Sealing had to be important, to hurt, to mean something. You don't cross your heart to be made a man's son! He knelt down—there were bits of flinty stone all over these hills. He looked for some but there were none up here. He crawled around, beginning to feel cold and stupid, pawing the grond, for a blade with which to sign himself in his pledge. At last he found a cow's tooth with part of it broken off jaggedly. He went back to where he had stood and held the tooth —over his head. "This stands for the knife in the cermony. It seals the oath."

Then he wondered where he should put the Sign. It was a thing to do over the heart, really, but he was accustomed to working with his shirt off sometimes, and it would be seen. His father would ask him what it was, and because it was his father asking, he wouldn't be able to lie. Where could he put the mark? Arms are seen. Legs and feet? Not dignified. The parts that are always covered are not decent anyway—it couldn't be anything below the waist. . . . He realized how little he could keep his secrets here, and for the smallest second before he quenched the disloyal thoughts, he was annoyed.

Finally he unbuttoned the top of his pants and, just below his navel, he began to scratch the shape of a cross. He worked hard because he felt stupid putting it there when he had wanted to put it over his heart in a place of dignity. He was also amazed that his flesh was so resistant. Once through the skin, he had somehow thought it would be easy, but the flesh fought his clumsy tool. When he thought he had done enough and that the mark was sure to stay, he buttoned his pants again and began to debate about the tooth. He didn't want to leave so symbolic a thing, but if he took it with him, it might be found, as his knife had been found. Finally he buried it on top of the hill and went back to the house tired, and at peace.

Schaller had seen him leave. He had heard a noise and awakened, gripped with a hard terror at the thought of his enemies closing upon him. Then he remembered Hobe and heard his footsteps padding downstairs, trying with ridiculous care to make himself quiet. Going to the backhouse, Schaller thought, but then in a few seconds he saw out of his window a patch of white moving quickly, and he sat up in bed and watched the boy running. What's he doing out there? Schaller wondered. There's nothing out that way but the barn. For a moment he sat rigid, seeing the picture of the boy continue in his mind. He must be going up to the barn for some reason. Running—it must be something important. What was he looking for? Not that fool knife of his—no, it must be something else.

There was a clear picture in Schaller's mind of his big barn looming up, dark, the boy running and the moon high and lonely over him. But the boy didn't go into the barn. He went around behind it. There was a minute and then he came back. He was holding something. Schaller looked hard at his picture—Hobe was holding the big garden fork and the post-hole shovel he had been using that afternoon. He was wiping them with a handful of hay to get the night dew off them so they wouldn't rust up. Then he was going into the barn to put them away.

Schaller sank down with a deep breath and turned back into his sleep. Later he half heard the boy coming back into the house and he was filled with a rare peacefulness. No hired boy he ever had took that kind of pride or that kind of care. The power of his own need had sent him someone who could help him stop the ravages of his tormentors, and then the whole house would sleep and there would be no more despair.

After that, and without any signals for beginning between them, Schaller and Hobe began to pour out words to each other. The talking came sporadically—it began from brief sentences at straightening up to ease a kink, between rows, a few words at rest before loading the pickup for town. Then they began to bring talk inside, sitting at the bare table and drawing in the crumbs. The mute farmer and the boy who envied muteness began to pour out the words of their misery. The boy spoke with merciless shame of his lavender aunts, the farmer of his poverty, the boy of his mocking schoolmates, the farmer of lies, the boy of his hunger to be free, the farmer of his hunger to be rich. At the height of their talking they sat for hours while old passions flickered across their memories.

One rainy day they stayed in and let everything go, and Schaller drew the shape of Koven and his plot and gave it the soul-crushing detail of all the years' entanglements: Koven at the stream poisoning the fish, Koven spooking every one of the turkeys to death, Koven's hypocritical sneering sympathy-play in town. Schaller connected past to present in great disjointed chunks—he was not used to speaking his thoughts—they veered and pitched from injury to injury, from recent past to dim past, from bitter present to inescapable future.

They both spoke, each in the thought that he was unburdening himself, each hearing in the other only what fed his own fires. Schaller listened to Hobe's misery at home and at school as a sign that he had made a man from nothing. It was so unlikely that a cripple-soul coward, a girl-boy like that could ever be changed, transformed, made a man, that what had happened must have been the action of some kind of mighty justice, some universal law to even things between himself and Koven.

Hobe heard in Schaller's words the profound truth of what the enemy world does to a hero. The fathers of the boys who wanted to break him were enviously trying to break Schaller. His answer to them was not one of fear now, but one of hate, and after that rainy day when Hoven's plotting was made plain, Hobe began to have bad dreams.

He had heard Schaller's words deeply and his dreams had Schaller's own symbols of The Enemy's gradual, relentless destruction—mice. The dreams began with pleasant scenes: He was captain of a long and graceful sailboat, tacking against the wind; a miner, stumbling upon a cavern of diamonds; a doctor saving; a soldier defending. The dream opened long, opulent vistas to him, and then, across one corner, hardly seen, one mouse, running. Soon another would go scurrying into the background, and then a third. The dream would limp on: successful campaign against the Indians, running the channel in his boat, all rip tides and white water; but soon there would be a sluggish weight in the boat and the sound of wood splintering under sharp teeth while he was a prisoner at the tiller. At the height of the Indian war, famine at the fort and out of nowhere, thousands of avid mice. Because the theme of mice never changed, Hobe soon saw these dreams as symbolic, mystifying stages on which the power of his enemies was played, one scene substituting for another. This knowedge that all the dreams, were, in effect, one dream, was more terrifying to him than if they had each been a different terror with a different meaning. One morning after a nightmare about being a powerful king at dinner—eaten by mice—Hobe took out the washstand drawer and killed the frantic mother who had given birth there. He considered this, quite properly, not done for himself but for Schaller, his father.

Hobe's ritual cut was troubling him. He had been forced to put it below his navel to avoid its being seen, but it was too close to his waist and sweat ran into it and stung him. When he worked hard, his pants slipped down, rubbing and chafing the cut until its inflammation turned into infection. Crusts formed and the sore drained from beneath them. He began to look around for something to put on the sore and finally he found some cow-salve. Schaller had few commercial products around the place, but this one had been given him to try and he had put it in the barn and forgotten about it. Hobe couldn't take the whole can—that would be stealing—but whenever he could, he would dip into it and take a curl of it in his hand to use for the two treatments a day that the label said. He walked around in a perpetual stink of sulphur, creosote, and several other ingredients, but Schaller never seemed to notice.

The summer was at its height and the brief burst of strength that Schaller had had when the boy proved out was fading. All around him the weeds were conquering his crops, the milk was scanty, the eggs had shells so fragile that more cracked than stayed whole.

And Koven was stealing from the very earth beneath him, leaching out the richness of his soil. In his short moments of youth he had relaxed and been clean in hatred, but the return of hopelessness was almost more than he could endure. He worked by rote. His muteness came back upon him, so that he couldn't even remember how he had come to spend whole days and evenings talking, even though it was with the single person he could trust. The boy really was like a son. When he thought about what Koven was doing now, his anger was for the boy. Hobe had promised to come back after the winter was over, and after those harpy aunts of his had satisfied the law. When he was sixteen, he would come to stay. Koven was trying to take the boy from him too; he could see that. When the farm was ruined, all the boy's work would be for nothing, his respect for simple work would die and the veneration he had for Schaller, a real farmer and a real man, would be killed. To be killed with a knife is a quick death. To be killed with failure—that's dying hard. And the boy would have nowhere to go.

They were chopping kindling for the stove and cordwood for the smokehouse. Schaller said, "I tell you, Hobe, you ain't got enough hate in you. Thinking about easy things is for pickin' tomatoes, but when you sickle off or when you chop wood, you got to hate. It gives you the strength you need." He laughed bitterly and said, "Think that's Koven's head you got on that stump."

The boy raised the ax, stretching over the trunk he was going to quarter. Suddenly he found himself almost lifted off the ground. The journey of the ax took him with it as if gravity had suddenly ceased to urge him to possession of the center of the earth. And he was hating. His hatred was so great that he lost a sense of himself; he brought the ax down, cleaving the log and burying the ax's great tooth in the stump beneath it. Afterward they had to work the head out.

Schaller looked at Hobe when they were finished and said, "You really do hate, don't you, son?"

"Yes, sir," Hobe said, and lowered his eyes. It wasn't his hatred that made him ashamed, but because a man's emotions should be deep, unshown and unknown, and Schaller could read him as if he were water.

Schaller was very deeply moved. He had forgotten most of what he had said to Hobe, how much he had give up of himself when his secrets were welling out in their time of confidences. He remembered talking and talking, but he didn't remember what he had said.

"Has he been around here bothering you—Koven?"

The words were slow and Hobe heard them, knowing that Schaller hadn't thought of the possibility before. He wanted to ease himself and be free; he found himself answering, ". . . Dreams . . . I have these dreams, and . . . and . . . There were mice in one of the drawers. . . . I think he put mice in there. . . ."

He knew even as he said it that Koven himself hadn't injected a drug into him to cause him bad dreams or put the mice in the drawer himself, but he felt that what he had said to his father was truer than an actual fact or physical gesture. Somehow, the presence of Koven had resulted in these things. That was the reality under the words. It made the words true.

"Now you know," Schaller said, and looked out over his run-down place that a lifetime of backbreaking work couldn't save from his enemies, "Oh, he heads it all right, Koven does, but he ain't the only one. He has others with him, working for him to take our house and land and everything they can. When I go to sell out, well of course he can get it all. The place'll go for taxes after they've stolen all they can. It's no more than what they did in the war."

The boy thought of Vietnam, not the war Schaller meant—World War II.

Schaller went on in a grim monotone, "It's a part of the reason they hate me—because I seen a lot and I know a lot of what they done. Take the war. There was a family name of Dunkle lived over west—up over the hill there. They was good folks, farm people, the whole family. Young Roy went off to war, got killed. Did them vultures wait? No sir. Koven an' his pals on the other side—them Latchoga farmers on their fat river land—they didn't wait six months before they was up to the place naggin' the old folks to sell. They pestered 'em into sellin' too; sellin' low. Now it's me they're after an' my part of this hill. That Koven, he's got a Valley man's greed an' a Hill man's patience. Twenty years he's waited and played me. I don't know if I should tell you this—you're a good boy, and you might as well know. He knows who you are, son, and why you're here. . . . More than that, he knows what kind of fella you are. . . ." Schaller stopped, wondering what was to be said about the pain that was tightening on them. "You see, this house ain't as high as his. He can look out over the rise from his place to ours. He must have seen you shapin' up good here, and then movin' upstairs, like kin. That wasn't in the plan. . . ." His voice trailed off. His mind was looking toward the house where Koven was sitting in judgment of them while his hired men worked his land. "The ways he uses ain't ways you can fight. God knows, I've come through hard days—crops failin', droughts, even fire. A man can fight what he can see. They know how I can fight. . . ."

Hobe looked out over the summer land and up where birds danced and played. "Why don't we kill him?" he asked. "Why don't we just kill him and be rid of his rotten ways forever?"

Both of them hung together in a hollow, dreamlike silence. Hobe had said what each had been whispering and answering in deep places of his private wishes; but with words said, it was as if they had taken on a power of their own; as if the words said were half the act. Hobe had seen enough movies to know that there were two kinds of murder—and that one was thought to be less evil than the other; but he had never known why until just now when he was halfway toward killing an enemy he hated. *He* would kill the Enemy, not Schaller. It came to him with a sureness that would never be spoken between them. It was to be this, and not the stupid and shameful cuts on his belly that would be the blood-oath, the seal of adoption between himself and his ordained father.

In passion a man is killed once; in planned death, many times. A real man is a powerful being; his pride and suffering are caught in a body, just like a woman's or a little baby's, but a man is more than that—his pride and suffering can transcend his body. Koven's evil had been strong enough to bring dreams, breed mice, suck the strength from the land; but now the minds of the Vengeant were moving to get their revenge. They had already begun to kill their enemy. Their hate would weaken him; their plan would seek him out and cripple him long before they walked up to his door and Hobe gave him his body's death.

"Let's get back to this chore," Schaller said, and looked at the boy with the first peaceful expression Hobe had seen in weeks; it was almost a smile. "There's time to talk about it later. After supper. In the cool."

They went back to their work.

Now that Koven had been killed once, his subsequent deaths were easier. For a full week they mulled over weapons, methods, times. They rode him down in the truck; they poisoned his well; they set fire to his place; they rigged comic-book pitfalls, traps, electrified wires for him to blunder into; but in the end, they admitted that what they wanted of Koven was a personal death, one dealt face to face from them to him, a death that he would meet alone as they had suffered everything from him alone.

"I figure it ought to be while the fair is over to town," Schaller said at last. "His men'll be at the fair and if we make it the night before the fair closes, that's when they're most likely to be down drunk an' not even showin' up back at the farm."

"Is it a big fair?"

Hobe felt a sudden desire to go. Less for the fun he could have than for the memory of having wanted to go so many times before. He had never been to a fair. Such places, his aunts had told him, were dirty, sleazy, and unsanitary places ("The men who stay around the fair grounds have Diseases, Hobart, terrible Diseases. How do you know that the balloons are not blown up by such men, men with Diseases?") Before the moment when his vow had made him a man, he would have wanted very much to go, and he still remembered wanting to. He knew Schaller and Schaller's son should think it a waste of time.

"It ain't too big," Schaller said. "The women take an' go to 'em with all their preserves an' things. They have produce shows and stock judging and there's a carnyval. The carnyval is a pitiful place. They got freaks to laugh at, poor loonies, ought to be in the asylum; they got naked girls to dance an' tease boys that can't do nothin' but hope an' old men that can't to nothin' but remember. When they got all your money, they pick up an' leave. If we have plans for the last day of the fair, I think you just ought to go."

It was a miracle. How could a person have everything? Was there so much in the world for him? A grown man's work to do, a father, and now, a fair.

"Not if you need me here," he said.

"I got a job for you to do at the fair. Koven may know you—he has his spyglass on us over here—but the rest of 'em wouldn't. You'd get by, where I'd be spotted. I want you to go to the fair on Tuesday. Hang around the stock and farm exhibits; go down to the displays they got an' stay by the places where they stand around talkin'. You'll be able to hear what they're plannin' and what they know about us."

He got up and rinsed his cup out at the sink and then he turned back to the boy. "It's a job for a man who uses his brains; not a job for a fool. Anybody can *hear*—it takes brains to *listen*. There's two ways of listenin'. You got to listen this time with your whole mind—everything you know. They ain't goin' to talk about their plans for us right out." He had to strain to make the boy understand. "You got to feel along in the talk for where the real meaning is."

But Hobe was still wrestling with his own picture of the world. Men were true and their talk was true and direct. It was the women, the women whose talk held secrets and wove all the subtle, strange imprisonments. Then his confusion was cleared. These men who were Schaller's enemies—they weren't real men; they were liars and secret poisoners. They were like women.

"Listen," Schaller said, trying to prove his case. "A man ain't likely to take to the thought that other men see him for a thief and a liar. He has to have a way to hide what's there an' that way is by puttin' a good name to the things he does. That way people will let him get away with most anything. A man don't say, 'I'm out to break Schaller an' get his farm.' A man says, 'In modern farmin' you got to consolidate your acreage and increase it an' mechanize to break even. Small holdin's, why they stand in the way of progress.' You hear 'em sayin' it all over town. Nobody has to say, 'Kill Schaller—starve out a neighbor.' Nobody says it, but the plan is there—the idea is there for you to hear if you just listen right. I tell you what. If you don't think you can follow deep down under the fancy talk, you just listen good an' come back here an' tell me what they said, an' I'll get down to the bottom of it soon enough."

"I'll listen, I'll listen good," Hobe said. "An' then we'll be ready." He felt clean and strong and heroic, and he would get to see the fair, too.

It was a test that showed Hobe how easy it was for him to waver, even when everything depended on him, even when the stakes were his father's happiness and his own future. A disease had broken out among the chickens, so Hobe left without asking Schaller for a ride into town. He walked to the highway and hitched rides to the fair. He had two dollars of his pay for eating and getting into the exhibits where he needed to be. He had come to examine the people at the fair, and his purpose was straight and clear. Pride made him stand straight like Schaller did, in the simple, lonely dignity of what he had to do.

But somehow it wasn't what he expected, and the difference threw him off. The fair was all children, laughing and running around the big central area; families strolling here and there to the exhibits; friends meeting and music blaring from loudspeakers set up at the tops of tents; and booths, and hawkers chanting rote things mechanically into the crowds. For a minute all the complexity and color confused him. Schaller and the secret stealing and Koven's plot seemed dwarfed by all the life and movement and gaiety of the fair. It occurred to Hobe that he hadn't spoken to anyone but Schaller since he had gone to work—it was almost three months now. How could he go about and listen in to conversations when he didn't know who Koven's friends were, and who—besides Koven —Schaller's enemies were? Living so closely with Schaller for these months, he had expected the fair to resembled Schaller's picture of it—pretense of fun, pretense of farm-machinery displays and jelly judging, stock and quilts—all for effect. Under it all, there was to be the sound, the smell, a something malevolent arming and readying, and groups of plotters meeting and speaking earnestly and parting with signs. Even in laughter there should run an innocent-appearing code through which the malice and evil of their plan could be heard.

Hobe looked, walked around the midway and paused and listened, but he didn't hear what was supposed to be there. He got himself something to eat and then went over toward the shed where the new machinery was being demonstrated. All around him were the families, eager and happy, trying nothing more crucial than decisions about where they should go first. It was hard to see them as parts of the whirpool in which he and Schaller were the core. Lost in the crowd, it was hard to see himself as brave and alone. Boys of his own age were still bigger than he, still parts of families in whose ways and choices they seemed to be involved. Hobe's parents had died in an automobile accident, and mention of their death by the aunts was always circled with a little silence because the accident involved speed and violence, things that had always seemed to them to be obscene and shameful. Of course they had never let him ride on anything fast or violent—no bicycles, roller skates, carnival rides, airplanes. He wrote to the aunts twice a week, telling them the lies they wanted to hear, and occasionally he sent them the money that silenced them. Speed and violence were going to be his now, as well as the strength and courage to kill and to be the equal of the father he had found after so much shame and humiliation.

He went into the Farm of Tomorrow exhibit and pretended to study the machines and displays until he found a place where he could stand without being noticed. People came in to see the exhibits and he listened to every word they said, trying to sift the life-and-death meanings from their brief, idle words. After a while it did seem to him as if the families were being used as some sort of disguise. They were the only ones who talked to one another about what they saw. Boys taking their girlfriends through talked about themselves; groups of friends talked about other people and things; and in some of these conversations, Hobe heard the things that Schaller might want him to remember and report. Three farmers went past him, one talking to the others as they looked casually at the automated cow-milker, "I tell you, I don't want to wait any more. The top men say we can do it with controlled prices. Well, we've tried doing it with prices and all that happens is that we let another season go by, hoping that something's got to give. I'm tired of waiting. I want action and results instead of promises!" It could be about Schaller. It could be part of that code. That conversation should be saved.

Hobe waited. People came and went. Another group of farmers passed with talk about "him and her," and a girl bitterly answering a boy: "Don't tell *me* about it. If you're going to do it, well do it. Everybody says it's the right thing!" After a while three boys walked through. They were about sixteen and one was telling the others, "What do you reckon he's going to do when he finds out?"

"Who cares? It'll be too late by then."

"Listen, the way he is, he's been asking for it."

Even reading the words Schaller's way, there were only a few conversation that seemed to be about them. All around Hobe the world was going on, full of people who really seemed unaware of the life-and-death struggle being fought at the last line of defense—his father's farm. He couldn't decide if this gave him comfort or pain. It seemed to him, when he heard Schaller talk, that Koven had the whole world hating and conspiring to destroy them. Now he saw that most of the people didn't know or care. Maybe if they did know—if he told them what was happening—they would see, as he had seen, and try to help. . . . His head began to ache with figuring and refiguring the secrets in all the talk of all these strangers.

He left the Farm of Tomorrow and wandered out on the sunny midway. He passed a girly show without interest and had a few throws at one of the toss-ball games presided over by a lackluster skeleton of a man. Then he saw the fortune teller's booth and the tattoo tent and his heart split with yearning. He had come with only two dollars. He wanted to have the spread eagle —lonely, proud, and triumphant, three colors—across his whole chest, but that was far more than anything he could spend. The Ship with Anchor was seven dollars. It was two dollars just for initials, and he had already spent almost a dollar on food and the toss-ball game. The fortune teller's sign said "Your Fortune 50¢"; but when he got up close, he saw that if you wanted the future you had to pay a dollar. He didn't have any past. He wouldn't pay a dime to see his aunts shaking their long fingers and pursing their mouths at him from the crystal ball.

He walked on down the midway feeling his freedom and happiness draining away. Rides he had heard about and been denied when he was nine or ten no longer appealed to him—everything he wanted now was too expensive. In the end he went on some of the children's rides, feeling stupid and out of place. He ate some more and then went to all the free exhibits except the women's. It shamed him that he would have been more knowledgeable among the preserves and sewing than he was among the produce or animal-husbandry sections. What disturbed him most was the way he had lost importance in the mill of bright, easy people all around him. It was because of poverty. He had been shamed, and his cause seemed shamed too. He tried to call back the old feeling of pride by saying in his mind: "I'm going to kill a man. In a couple of days, I'm going to kill a man." It didn't sound important. It had lost its stature in the blare of calliope music.

At sundown he hitched a ride to the highway cutoff with a big, loud-laughing family. They cackled away during the whole trip and he would have written them off as foolish and useless except that their boy, Tom, who was his own age, was bigger than he.

He went home in the near dark. walking the two

miles from the cutoff under a lumpy, misshapen moon. He had felt so lucky to be going to the fair. Now he was coming back two dollars poorer, with a headache and a sick feeling of having lost something of value.

About halfway home, he remembered that Schaller was going to be waiting for his report. He went back in his mind confidently, reaching for all those secrets he had heard at the stalls and along the midway. There were no secrets. He stopped, startled, and then tried with increasingly frantic sweeping of his mind to conjure up the faces he had seen and the words he had heard. He tried remembering where he had stood so as to bring back the speakers as they had walked past him. He saw the lovers vaguely, and their lips were moving, but they were not the people whose words he needed. He brought back the three men, but their talk was not clear. Something about prices was all he could remember, but not exactly what they had said. There were some boys too, and a "he" who might have found out something, but there was no plan, no proof, no statement that wasn't a vagrant wisp to blow away in a minute and leave him with nothing. What was worse, he had had moments all day when his cause and Schaller's had seemed as vague. People weren't looking at or scheming or worrying about Schaller's successes or failures, his victory or the bitter horror of his defeat. They were doing something worse, really; they were unconcerned. They didn't care at all. He shivered. All alone, he thought. Nobody is trying to remember *our* faces, or what *we* say. Nobody thinks about *us*.

Overhead the vast sky swam. It was unconcerned. The earth on which he and Schaller worked, lay heaped around him. Wasn't it important that they were fighting to close its wounds and pull a farm from the small ground that lay between its rib-bones? The sky and earth were measured in millions of years, and nobody cared about Schaller and his son planting, weeding, working, and going to their ruin.

He had passed Koven's place hardly noticing the light. He heard small animals in the brush beside him and wondered if snakes would lie in the road at night to get the warmth the sun had left there. He began to peer ahead at the bumps and potholes in the road, trying to read intelligible shapes of them the way Schaller would be waiting to read the words he had collected. At last he came to the rut that Koven had put in the road. It startled Hobe that the shadow in its hollow should seem to be its form. It made him uncomfortable like the funny mirrors he had passed at the fair. He hadn't stopped in front of them or posed like the others who passed by. Things should mean what they mean and be what they are. If a person could look one way to himself and another way to a stranger, how could he really tell who he was? What was to stop a person from seeing everything differently from the way it really was? He didn't like to think about a life that could be seen differently from mirror to mirror. He turned in home and was warmed by the comfort of light shining from the kitchen and coming in a muted glow through the uncurtained front-room windows. All its bleakness was lost in the forgiving night; the conquering weeds, the weathered fencing, all the sagged, broken, wornout things that surrounded them all day were erased, forgiven. Only the warm, peace-promising light remained. He went toward it, stopped, and began to tremble. He didn't deserve the light or the father who sat waiting in the light for him.

He had been disloyal, slipping into questions and suspicion the minute he was away from the farm. He had actually wondered if Schaller couldn't have been wrong about the plans against him, and about all the people who were in league with Koven. "But I've come back," he whispered to himself. "I did come back. Take me in." The house and the light accepted him, and Schaller too, in a kindness that made Hobe grateful for the small lit kitchen after eternity, the night, and the stars.

In bed Hobe marveled at the length of the awful day of testing through which he had come. Still, he had come through it, strengthened in the truth. He had learned his lesson. He would never doubt again.

When they talked the next day, Schaller was pleased. He hadn't questioned Hobe immediately and he saw now that it had been wise to wait. He'd had twenty years of practice, listening, hearing what went on in people's minds and carefully fitting what they said to what they really meant. Putting a kid to a problem like that, even a kid as smart as Hobe, was asking a lot. All those sounds and arguments and lies to sift and sort could weigh down hard on someone who wasn't used to it. Hobe had come home exhausted; he could see that, but slowly, in the bend and rise of their work, bit by bit, the words would come back to the boy.

As they weeded the next day, Schaller began to bring Hobe around to talking about the fair, and with a deftness strange to him, he slowly led to the people at the fair and soon some of the words came back to Hobe and he set them before Schaller gratefully. He was repaid, forgiven.

With astonishing skill, Schaller took the few words and fitted them into the plan that Koven and the others had against them. Hobe was amazed at how surely and neatly they fit, and Schaller was pleased, seeing Hobe's admiration for the intricate work of his mind. "You see, I never would have listened to the young ones—them boys you heard. It's the older ones—men Koven's age I would have paid mind to. I see I done right sendin' you along. Boys, they're more likely to be loose-lipped. It's no surprise the men would get their kids into it. You done right listenin' to the boys. As I think about it more, I figure the boys would be doin' more of the actual work of all this, and the older men makin' the plans."

"Does Koven have a boy?" Hobe asked, and Schaller saw into his mind where they were squaring off, man versus man, boy versus boy. He still saw Koven as only a man, like any other. "No," he said, "he had a wife, but she died. They never did have no children. Koven ain't breakin' me for some natural thing like a son. He wants the power and the land for a reason we ain't even guessed at. The men in them Latchoga farms down there in the valley—they got common men's reasons. With me gone they can fix their own prices an' make college boys out of their kids an' be like kings down there." He stood straight and looked at Hobe who had begun to pack the early apples in bushel baskets. The apricots and cherries and peaches had come and gone; tomatoes and peas and beans and radishes and dill and cucumbers for canning had been picked and sorted and sold. Summer was ending. He could feel it in his body and soul as if the blood were draining away.

"Before the fair, you said somthin' about Koven—about killin' him."

The boy's eyes flickered. Hadn't it all been planned, all sure? Hobe had a terrible sinking fear, suddenly, that Schaller hadn't heard him or had forgotten all those days of plans and weapons. He could barely murmur, "Yes."

"They say," Schaller went on, "that women are the ones who change their minds. They do say so, and I reckon it's true—a woman doin' that—yet I wouldn't hold it against a man that he had to do it. Women don't need reasons to change, but a man, well, he might have all kinds of reasons to say a thing and then change his mind. . . ."

Hobe felt for the first time that he was being led by Schaller, but the words themselves made sense to him. What reason could he give that would be a reason of a brave man? They had decided it already, and he had already lived in hope of it. It was to be the day when by act not symbol, he would hear the heavy word "Man" from Schaller's mouth. He would be a man and a son by blood trial and blood tie.

"I have changed my mind," Hobe said slowly, so there would be no mistaking his words. "I don't want to shoot him; I want to face him clean and kill him with my knife."

"Bless you, son," Schaller said.

They spent the next day planning. The moon would help the boy to see, but he would have to be quick and not so late that Koven's men would be back from the fair. If Hobe hid in the barn, he could be there when Koven went to check on his stock. Hobe would take his knife, but he would also take something from the barn wall in case Koven saw him first and attacked him and there wasn't time to face him with the knife. Schaller dwelt on the method Hobe must use in order to kill. Hobe hung to the stinging words of truth which he would say, and which would reduce Koven to terror and shame before he was killed. When his words had been said, death would be a blessing.

"If you're gonna use that knife"—Schaller kept intruding—"you'd better know how to use it. You have to get up to his heart without it hittin' bone, right up under his ribs." Schaller had an idea that he should tell Hobe how easy it was to kill. He felt confident and proud of this strong, brave boy whom he had raised. He was easy in his mind now; he talked about the hogs he had slaughtered, and the cows too, and how killing was as much a routine of bend and straighten as pulling corn. Hobe listened, but his real thoughts were on the words of Koven's death, which he had already begun.

When the night came, they stopped talking about Koven altogether. They drew into a complete, silent camaraderie, moving together through their work and their meal as if they were a single being. They seemed to hear each other's needs in the silent closeness that flowed between them. The moment that Schaller reached for the salt, Hobe brought it to his hand. The moment that Hobe felt weariness, Schaller rose and began to turn out the lights. They checked the barn together, moving closely in the same rhythm, and the silence in their minds was peace.

They worked all the next day cleaning out the barn. Their silence fed them through the hot, stinking fly-buzz noon. They worked in a long, rhythmic unison, sensing where to help each other and how to move in the pace that kept them almost touching but never in each other's way.

Hobe had never known such happiness. That his own stringy body had given him this gift filled him with awe. That Schaller's idea of sonship was such simple, perfect equality overwhelmed him with gratitude. No wonder he had failed so often before. Without the nourishing strength shared with a true father, the world was a seething mass of enemy strangers. It was true what Schaller said about the world. Koven and the men in the valley were trying to destroy his father through robbery, just as the boys at school had been trying to destroy him with laughter. There was something those boys hadn't counted on. Hobe would be back after this summer. He would come back a son, someone with strength and anger instead of shame. Let them call him baby girl and sissy now. He worked with his father, breathing in time, not hurrying. The night would come and he would be ready. Of that he was sure.

They ate early, sitting peacefully at their food and saying little. At sundown, Hobe got up from the table and went for his knife, leaving the house as if on an ordinary errand. He walked west, letting the darkness overtake him, going a long way around so as to get to Koven's barn without passing the house.

Schaller stayed, waiting. Never had his mind been so still. The voices of shame were gone; his own words of anger and despair were silent. How strange and wonderful it was that the source of all this change was the little weakling runt he had picked up at the train station in the spring! Hobe was strong and confident now, and after tonight—after tonight—neither of them would have to stand stiff as ramrods because of Koven's spyglass that was always on them. After tonight, the valley men wouldn't be able to set prices to suit themselves. He would be what they were—only more. The reward goes to the man who works for it and he had worked, God knows. After tonight, the stolen years would be repaid. In his mind, he saw himself and Hobe walking in bright sunshine together, and sharing the peace of summer evenings over all the years that seemed perpetually spring. If they wished to listen to the thoughts of people who passed by the house or were envious of them from dark corners, the thoughts would pour out to them full of adulation and reverence. He sat at the table dreaming; he didn't notice the darkness or the passage of time, and so he was surprised when Hobe came in and turned on the lights. In the sudden glare, shocking the eyes, Hobe looked sick and pale. He moved like a ghost. He was covered with blood.

Hobe lay in bed and tried to feel something deep and symbolic about where he had been and what he had done, but he kept misplacing the event, having to drag it back and think about it. In the movies, men, even villains, were racked by guilt, or else they exulted and felt powerful. Nobody just forgot, nobody just lost in the mass of details a murder he had done. He would have to confess the most shaming of these details to Schaller tomorrow. It made him squirm in bed to think of how awful that part had been. How would he be able to tell his chosen father that fear in the end had made him kill so stupidly and wildly? There he'd been in the barn, waiting until he could hardly bear it. His muscles got cramped and sore from holding that waiting posture so tensely. His knife was ready, his hate was ready, and the ax that Schaller had told him to take from the barn wall was ready in his hand. When the barn door opened, a spring inside him was touched and released, and he leaped from his hiding place with such fury that he almost fell before he reached Koven, reached him not with his knife, not his bitter words that were to bring humiliation before death, but with the ax, the brute weapon. He fell on Koven, his raised arm came down with the action of his falling and the ax found itself buried in Koven's head. The man had not uttered a sound or taken a step into the barn. Hobe's thrust had pushed him back through the doorway into the moonlight and there he lay. Strange to think about it—they had never planned further than the murder itself. All the words that Hobe was going to say, all the judgments he was going to call down had been cut off by the falling of the ax, and it had been in fear alone, plain coward fear. He had landed on top of Koven by the power of his leap, and looking into Koven's face, he had been amazed at how closely the man resembled Schaller in the moonlight. It was more than their ages. He had expected Koven to be fat and insolent like the mice that lived so well on Schaller's stolen grain and licked the butter from his tubs. Koven had the same stringiness and the same straightness that Schaller had. The man himself was so different from Hobe's picture of him that for a long moment Hobe was afraid he had killed one of the hired men.

A dog had come trotting gracelessly up to where the body lay. The dog sniffed, licked at the man's face and began to whine. Hobe didn't know what to do. He was afraid that the dog would attack him if he touched the man. He hadn't counted on there being a dog at all. He got up slowly and began to walk away a step at a time. The dog paid no attention to him.

When Hobe came in sight of Koven's house, he saw a light in a room downstairs. Without knowing why, he started to walk up to the house. Something made him sure that nobody else was there. The light was coming from the kitchen. He could see the stove and part of the wall near it. The wall was like the one he looked at every day at Schaller's—the same calendar from the First National Bank. He had seen the saccharine picture so often he had to laugh in the dark. *School's Out*. The same sicky, empty-faced boy was carrying books for the same sicky-empty-faced girl. There was a little tin match holder, compliments of the hardware store. The same. It was tacked up just where Schaller's was. Hobe didn't know why, but it frightened him. He turned away and walked back over toward the western part of Koven's land. The sound of the dog's whining reached him and then faded. Toward the top of the hill he stumbled in some downed barbed wire and had to work himself free. Something was weighing on his mind, something the shape of which he couldn't quite catch away from darkness. It vibrated at the rims of his thoughts, but as soon as he tried to light it, it retreated from him. It reminded him of the rut that Koven had put in the road, and that he had seen walking home from the fair. The shadow in it had seemed to be the shape of something lying there; the hump, in the play of light, had seemed to be flat. He didn't like to think about it.

In another minute he was at the top of the hill. He stopped then and looked around. He could see both farms from where he stood. The night was very still and the moon bathed houses, land, and trees in an equal light. All the fields and buildings made a pattern in the moonlight. Both farms were quiet; they might both have been sleeping or deserted, but he knew. Nobody in the world—not even Schaller—knew what he knew. He began to go down the slope toward Schaller's; then, crossing the stream, he suddenly realized how cold the night was. Autumn was coming. It didn't matter—he was home.

Eager as children they woke to their new day. The sun was shining, the sky an unequivocating deep blue. Koven's diseased hand had fallen away from the farm, the spying eye was blank, the lying tongue dried over. The whole world seemed washed, ready and new. Schaller and Hobe weeded and fixed fences and put new chicken wire in the poultry run, knowing that a weed pulled today would not be replanted in the night, the fresh wire would not be rusted or cut into, the fences not pulled down. Milk seemed more plentiful, cream yellower, the eggs better already. The wind that blew over the hill was eager and quickening with the first edge of autumn in it. After lunch Hobe washed his clothes and Schaller gave him some lye water for the stains. While the clothes were drying, Schaller got Hobe a shirt and overalls of his own, and Hobe wore them happily, smelling his father's smell on them. Father and son stopped work sometimes just to look toward the north where the wind captured hill after hill with a swell like the sea, and they were both tired and happy. They had worked like six; they had done it easily; they congratulated themselves on the progress they had made. There was no mention of Koven, how he had died or when, no word except the always unspoken, clean, male joy reminding them that his death had freed them and their land.

The next day was lowering and dark. Hobe was pruning back a cherry tree when a branch gave and threw him off balance. He fell from his ladder in a shower of leaves and twigs, managing to catch the tip of his saw on the side of his head as he went down. He landed flat, the breath knocked out of him, and he lay in rising and falling waves of nausea until Schaller came by and found him. They were reeling together toward the house when a jagged lightning tore its stitches out of the sky, a crack of thunder followed, and a torrential rain began.

They got to the porch and stood looking at the wild, destroying rush of wind, and at the rain that rode upon it as if for vengeance. Schaller kept shaking his head; his teeth were gritted and he was murmuring over and over, "Damn you, Koven. . . . Damn you, Koven. . . ."

Hobe's head was pounding. He wanted to tell Schaller that Koven was dead, that even if the shadows of his hatred were still falling across the farm, the awful presence behind them was gone. But even breathing hurt him and he was still threatened with terrible nausea, so he didn't trust himself to speak. After a while they both sat down and rested. There was nothing to do but watch the rain beat down what they had planted. They heard shingles tear on the roof; fences fall; foliage go down; doors slam, swing, slam; and finally tear away.

In an hour the rain calmed to a drizzle and then stopped, leaving a lurid white sky in the north. They went out to survey the damage. Hobe was still weak, but he followed along as well as he could, marveling that weeds always thrived while the planted, needed, tended crops were caught and torn by every wind and sucked by every drought.

After a while, Schaller sent him to see if any large branches had fallen in the road. Hobe was shivering as he looked through the brush. He was so tired that only with great effort could he make himself understand what he saw, and he spent long minutes looking stupidly down the road. He thought he heard water running somewhere and he walked toward the sound. It was Koven's rut; the rut that Koven had dug in the road. It was pouring muddy water, eroding its banks and deepening itself with the runoff. He stared at it dumbly for a while and then he walked over to the side of the road looked through the undergrowth from where the water was coming. It was coming from the stream. It was only from the stream. At one time or another, that stream, in which there had once been fish, had overflowed its bank by the side of the road and had made itself a little runnel across the road right by Schaller's property line. Successive storms must have deepened it and Schaller, thinking it was Koven's doing, had never examined it to see what had happened.

Hobe walked down to where the stream turned and went along Koven's property line. It was true. The outermost bank had all washed away and now the overfilled stream was seeking the deeper channel, the one that went across the road at Schaller's line. All at once Hobe couldn't endure his chill and nausea. He stood gaping at the running water, the turn of the stream, the eroded place, as if they were miracles or sick dreams in his own mind. He remembered in a wave of dizziness that he had first heard Koven's name in connection with the rut in the road on the first day that he had come. Now summer was over, and he was Schaller's son, and Koven was lying dead just outside his barn, probably in water because of the rain. It must have rained on Koven's place too. The thought shocked him. He started to turn back, but the world turned instead and he saw the ground beginning to rise and turn. He had no perception of falling.

Schaller called and called and finally found Hobe all the way down the road near Koven's. He wondered what had happened to make him pass out on the road like that and then he remembered the fall he had had. There he was all the way down by Koven's, going back to the scene, maybe; back there to check on things, or else maybe to get his knife if he'd left it behind. "Good thing you didn't go," he said to the heap, and then he bent down and lifted the still very light boy in his arms.

The day had been awful, as bad as a day under Koven's eye, and especially bad after yesterday, the day of peace and promise, when they had seemed to be free at last and forever. What if Koven's eye hadn't been shut after all? What if it was still on them? What if the boy had only wounded him and left him for dead? . . . No, Hobe had had a sureness about him. . . . What if he only thought he had killed Koven— that stupid knife of his might go in flesh up to the hilt and not kill a man; and the boy had no experience with killing. They hadn't said a word about it since Hobe had come back. There would have to be words said now.

Hobe slept all afternoon and by evening he was better. They were quiet, eating, but not with the silent sense of union they had shared before. After they finished, Schaller stood up and waited for Hobe, but Hobe was a little slow. Pain was beginning in his whole body from the strain of the fall. Schaller threw his spoon on the table. "I'll have to ask you—did you kill him?" For a minute Hobe didn't understand the question. "Are you sure he's dead!"

Then, Hobe remembered that he had killed Koven,

and he answered laconically, in the way he had hoped to answer all this time, "The ax was halfway through his head. If it didn't kill him, it slowed him some."

He was all ready to laugh until he looked up and then corrected himself numbly, shocked by the rage he saw in Schaller's face. "I killed him, sir, he's dead. He didn't move or breathe. I left him dead, sir." Then he took another breath. It was time to admit his shame, that he hadn't used the knife at all. "I couldn't get to use my knife—to tell him we had his number and knew what he was doing and were going to make him pay. I killed him with the ax, not the way we wanted . . . and I thought you should know."

He waited in the silence and then moved and heard his own foot rasping the dirty floor.

Schaller looked at him steadily and said, "He's dead, ain't he?"

Hobe looked down and didn't know whether Schaller was telling him that men never cry over what they have done, or beg, or plead for approval, or that he didn't care if Koven was killed a man's way or not. Hobe suddenly had a picture of the rut and the pouring water, and later he wouldn't be able to tell whether he had begun to speak in bitterness or as a son. "Oh, and—I found out about where the rut comes——" Something made him stop. He didn't know why. He had sworn to have no other loyalty, no other secrets, but a hand had come to cover his mouth before the words could be formed. Then suddenly, another idea appeared before him and he accepted it blindly. "—— where the house comes. . . ." He was suffering a strange self-consciousness, and that he had taken the wrong way was made plain to him when it was too late to guard his tongue. "Koven's house. The hill is too close to the house—I mean that Koven's house is lower and there's the hill, close——" Schaller was standing still, looking down at him curiously, waiting for him

to make sense. "I mean, sir, we thought that Koven
was spying on us. He must have looked from some
other place, because his house is really lower, quite a
bit lower than ours, and the hill is there and shuts
out his view." The same silence was all that came to
him. He said, "Maybe he did it some other way . . .
from the road; or maybe he had a special place built
on top of the barn—I don't remember the top of his
barn . . . he might have had something on top of the
barn . . . for . . . him . . . to sit on. . . ."

Schaller seemed not to have heard him at all. He
took a cigarette out of his pocket and lit it and then
said, "You had a bad fall there today. You should get
to bed, get some rest. We got a hard day tomorrow,
cleanin' up after the rain. I'll close up."

Hobe thanked him, but Schaller didn't seem to hear.
His eyes were looking past Hobe and his mind was
with something at which Hobe could only guess. He
went upstairs to bed, numb with loss.

The next day Koven's dog came around. It was a
lumpy, grizzled dog, its legs stiff with arthritis. It circled the house, whining and yelping, moving in closer
each time. When they noticed it, Hobe knew it must
be traveling around to the neighbors for food. Koven
had been dead almost three days. The dog's hunger
had driven him away from his master. The dog seemed
to show no special recognition of Hobe. It came toward
him in its stilted way, puffing with exertion and whining now and then. He went toward it to pet it and it
licked his hand, shaking in a stiffened way. "You sure
are an ugly old dog," Hobe said. "It's a wonder he
kept you all this time. . . ." The hand came down
again to cover his mouth, but this time it was less adept
at stopping the words in his mind. An arthritic ugly
old dog like that wasn't like the dogs villains are supposed to have. Evil men had evil dogs, big snarling

mastiffs, killer watchdogs on silent paws. He thought of himself going over to kill Koven, not even knowing he had a dog, and what if it had been a big, vicious dog and attacked him? Stupidly, he began to tremble about the nonexistent watchdog springing at him from an unhappened darkness. Schaller came up to stand by him. He said quietly, "You're gonna have to kill that dog."

It brought Hobe out of his daydream. "Sir?"

"I said, you're gonna have to kill that dog."

Hobe looked up at Schaller in wonder. "But he's just an old dog—why don't we keep him? We could feed him and keep him, maybe, an' in the winter——"

"That is Koven's dog!"

"But he's just a sick old dog—it's been three days since he's eaten——"

"We feed him and he'll hang around here stealin'. Don't you think Koven taught him to steal? How do we know it ain't been this dog stealin' from us? If you won't kill him, I will. I goin' up to the barn and get my gun."

While he was gone, Hobe tried to get the dog to go away. He didn't dare yell or throw a stone, for fear that Schaller might be looking.

Of course Schaller had good reasons for not wanting to keep the dog. It might bring suspicion on them. Hobe knew a lot of mystical things about dogs. He had heard how they walked across the country to be with their masters, pointed out killers to the police, traced people by scent and sound. Even a sick old dog like this one might know how to do all these things, biding its time and waiting to bring the killer to justice. But a dog wouldn't be loyal to a man like Koven. It's a scientific fact that if a dog likes a man and stays with that man, then there is bound to be good in that man. Hobe put a lot of weight in the instincts of animals. All he could do was gesture the dog away, snarling in and undertone and whispering, "Get out! Go on!" The dog tipped its head to one side and stood looking at him as he gesticulated. Then Schaller came down from the barn with his gun. He moved toward the dog and the dog moved away, wagging its lumpy tail slowly. Schaller moved again. The dog backed away. Schaller raised the gun, grappling with the stiff trigger. The dog turned and trotted slowly off toward the road. Schaller adjusted his aim, but the dog disappeared into the undergrowth that lined the road. A truck rattled by and Schaller was afraid to shoot—and then the dog was gone. "Damn him! Damn that Koven!"

When they were sweeping up fallen branches for the woodpile and compost heap, Hobe began to wonder about the old dog. He couldn't get the thought of Koven and a dog off his mind. "That sure was an ugly old dog," he said.

Schaller grunted.

"I wonder how long that old dog was with him."

"How should I know? I didn't have no spyglass trained on him all day from my bedroom, like he had on me."

"I didn't mean that—I thought you might have seen him in town."

"I changed my days—he goes—he went in town Tuesdays and Saturdays, mostly. I wouldn't be seen near him. I changed my days. After the war he got that nice new pickup, makin' money out of the war. I quit talkin' to him since then. I changed my days so's I wouldn't run into him in town."

Hobe clicked his tongue. "A man who makes money off a war is no good," he said firmly.

Koven's house might be lower, and he might not have dug the rut across the road, but he had been a traitor anyway, a man against his country.

"Oh, he had a thousand ways," Schaller said, warming in Hobe's disapproval. "Everyone lived a little scarce durin' the war days—it was the patriotic thing; gettin' your shoes fixed again 'stead of buyin' new, for instance. Not Koven, not him. He managed to get all kinds of new extra shoes out of them rationin' books."

Rationing books? There were no rationing books except in one war. Hobe opened his mouth to ask about them, but hopelessly his mind betrayed him with memory and he saw himself again standing in the moldering past of his aunts' attic, the open trunks spilling hideous clothes. They had been saved there. The Second World War was "their" war, a war as antique and dry as they were. And it was this war which was Schaller's war and Koven's. Hobe had never realized that his new father and his old aunts shared a tie as strong as a war—a real war with rules and ration books. "I saw some of those books once," he said weakly.

Schaller mistook the source of his confusion. "Oh, it wasn't so bad." He opened again to the boy's sympathy. "Only because of the ones that cheated, a lot of us got short on things. Koven, he always had new things nobody else could get in them days—new pair of shoes every time you looked around. I didn't hold with it. I quit talkin' to him. An' then, right after the war he got that new truck. What kind of man is that, proud to be rich off all the killin'? That truck was runnin' on soldiers' blood. I changed my days, like I told you."

It meant the truck was bought in 1946. It meant Schaller hadn't spoken to Koven since 1946. Hobe had a sinking feeling. He picked up a load of leaf trash and staggered with it to the compost pile. Schaller's hate suddenly seemed as ancient and dry as the dusty ration books, his fear for the land something out of an old man's querulous feud. But anyway, the desperate mind cried, Koven had been a traitor. Schaller must have known his plans some other way. Anyway what difference did it make! He and his father had been close once, and now there was closeness missing. He had to bring it back. The only way to do this was with work. He had proven himself once by his work and he would have to do it again.

He thought that maybe down deep in his mind, he had wanted thanks for what he had done. Maybe that was the trouble. Thanks and proofs of love were for his aunts. He hated their demands of gratitude from him ("Why don't you wear your Christmas sweater, Hobart? You know I made it myself. . . .") Work had saved him once, given him a father and a future and a tough, strong body. It would save him again. He picked up the pitchfork and went back for another load, a double load this time.

He worked at his salvation. He worked until he was exhausted and beyond exhaustion. He worked in a desperate mill of despair like a beaten prizefighter who flails for the opponent he can no longer see. He denied his body, but his mind would not bend to the discipline. His thoughts began to be like reflections in the fun-house mirrors at the fair. They swelled and shrank, bloated and shriveled before him. One minute a thing would seem reasonable and clear; the next, disjointed, misshapen, fantastic. Once when he and Schaller were getting eggs, he noticed the delicate way that they had to reach into the nests, thumb and forefinger like ladies selecting little cakes at a fancy tea. It made him break into a wild, ungovernable laughter, and when Schaller asked him what was funny, he couldn't stop laughing to tell him. Schaller grumbled that he was gettin brain sick. "That fall rattled your head. You been goin' on about all kinds of things since you fell out of that tree. If you're finished with your cat-fit, you can put in some more work."

But Schaller was more frightened than angry. Omens were gathering around him and they were pointing toward something yet more horrible than the years of Koven's cunning. Hobe had fallen out of a tree and hadn't been the same since. The ckickens were still sick, and earth still poor. He began to wonder if Koven hadn't been some kind of a barrier between him and the evil of the rest of them. Maybe Koven had stood there separating him from the world's hate, filtering through only so much as his enemy could take, and absorbing the rest with his all-powerful body. How could that storm have come if it hadn't been an omen too? After the storm Hobe had started to ask all those questions. Once the boy had made believing as real as food or sleep. Now he was laughing like a crazy girl, at nothing, saying, "Don't kill Koven's awful, guardian dog." "Where else could Koven have spied from since his house was lower?" Great God, hadn't he seen that spyglass himself, sliding the sun off it when it turned, just a white-hot glint and then gone? Why did Hobe deny it? Why were there just the days now? The days fell, indistinguishable from all the others that had burned away his years. Weeds conquered, silt conquered, weathering and worms conquered and were insolent in their victory. Lightning had walked down one of the fruit trees, burnt clear through to the heartwood and sizzled the sap to black crystals in it. An omen! In the evening he sat in his kitchen, bolt upright in the chair until bedtime, because he didn't know what move he could make now to bring back the land, the farm, his days of strength.

One evening as he was sitting that way, holding on the table, a huge, complacent rat came out of the pantry, looking at him without the slightest trace of fear. It walked across the room and past him, seeking no safety, not breaking stride. An omen!

Schaller had never had nightmares. Now they came one after the other, explicit and terrifying.

Koven was dead, one with the earth, and so part

of earth and air, water, and fire. He had made Hobe describe Koven lying dead on the ground outside the barn. The rain had come and beaten his elements into the earth. Rats had come and gnawed at his face and taken his element to nourish them and their race forever. Koven alive had been a giant, a dark, brooding monster. Now he was of the land, of the night, of the sun and the wind, and in all of them now, was His Plan.

Hobe had caused this. Hobe had made it happen— his own son. In the nightmares, Schaller's forgotten church sounded echoes from the ancient days. Schaller had forgotten most of his religious teachings. He had stopped going when his mother died in 1936, but he remembered the words of scripture because of their mystical power. Now in dreams Body and Blood were his—or Koven's. The Son betrayed The Father, and Judas was the power that overflowed the world.

From sunup to sundown, Hobe worked without stopping, trying to show his father that Koven was dead. He went on like an automaton, with little food or rest. The work must show the father a great redeeming fact, and that fact would be a whole life saved. He cut huge fields of weeds. All around the house he trimmed and neatened. He nagged Schaller into let him paint the house and barn, and he painted the front façades first so that whenever Schaller came back from town, he would drive into his place and see it new and shining all at once. One afternoon when Schaller thought Hobe was working on the back of the barn, he crept down and filled in the rut in the road and rebuilt the creek bank so it wouldn't overflow again.

In his desperation he did not let himself see that the farm's salvation was beyond his strength. Even the house took endless days to paint. It had weathered twenty-five years of time without help, and all the while he was standing tiptoe on ladders or hanging precarious-ly upside down from the roof to get the small triangle under the eaves, the weeds grew and kept growing, other wire netting was breaking, other rotted boards fell off. Only when his aunts wrote to him that school was going to start next week, that he must come home immediately, did he stop, look around, and see that he was lost and helpless, out of strength, out of time, drowning. He reached for Schaller to be his hope.

"I got two coats on the front of the house and one on the front of the barn. The weeds won't be so bad around the house next year, an' I'll be back up first thing in the spring, an' you don't have to worry about me keepin' up. I'm gonna exercise regular in the gym and that way I'll be able to start right in."

"You think we're gonna have a farm next year? What makes you think there's gonna be anything left up here?" Schaller was sitting at the table. His face was empty and there was a vagueness about his move-ments that disturbed Hobe more than what the old man actually said. For days he had done chores and not much else, wandering here and there, picking up a tool and putting it down again without purpose.

Hobe had fought for his father and had not given up. Fighting was a new truth for him, a truth proven, and he wouldn't renounce it. "Next summer, we'll be *startin'* without him, all the way from the beginning. We'll have months to get the farm back up in tip-top shape, and you'll still have the winter . . . all the repairs he tore out. . . . Everything is gonna last now. . . ."

His wall of talk was to keep chaos back. He couldn't hold up the wall. Schaller's face crumbled, the hands plucked at crumbs on the table. He was crying. It wasn't the thick-voiced clearing of the throat that even the stone men in movies allowed themselves in the great moments when they had to show they weren't stone after all. It was a dry, wrenching series of sobs through which Schaller tried to speak like a little child or a woman. "All . . . alone. . . . All alone. . . . Nobody left. Nothing . . . left. . . ."

Hobe fled in shame and disgust. Only later when he found that Schaller had moved his things back to the "hired man's" room, did he realize Schaller hadn't been crying for the loss of a son, but for the loss of an enemy.

The next day Schaller was going into town and Hobe asked him to pick up a train schedule. The farmer nodded but said nothing. When he left, Hobe packed and sat waiting. He knew there was work to do while Schaller was gone. The intimacy he had with the workings of the farm gave his mind's eye all the range and detail of things left undone: the last unpainted window frame, the scum to be cleaned from the trough where the animals drank, the hole in the barn floor that he had meant to fix last week. He also hoped dumbly that Schaller would come home changed again, that there had been some reason for all the evil and anguish that had settled on their house, a circumstance to answer and forgive it all.

For a while he stared into space, remembering the brightness and beauty of his coming of age. He remembered how they had worked together, the honor of sleeping like a son upstairs, the way their hands and bodies had moved in a rhythm that gave their work the grace and strength of an art, come by in blood, love, and patience. And their minds had spoken together, almost as a person would think to himself, half without words.

All that was before Koven died. The night he had gone to Koven's was the last beautiful night. He remembered climbing back up the hill afterward in the watering moonlight that shimmered on the long grasses. It was a strange feeling to remember what it was like when he looked into Koven's kitchen and saw everything almost as if it were Schaller's. His mind caught on it for a moment and then fled in terror, pulling him out of his daze in a startled rush from truth.

He tried to outrun the meaning of the pictures he had just seen, but they caught him at last and overwhelmed him. Koven's kitchen, so much like Schaller's; the downed barb wire on the hill, the look of the barn, the overgrown grasses all around. Koven had no hired men, no vast wealth, no spies, no road-rut, no trained mice, no spyglass, no midnight fence-breakers, no topplers of stones, no poisoners of fish. They were two old men farming hate because it was all that could grow on their leached-out land. He sat on his chair, dumb. Time passed. He didn't move. A car drove up and he wasn't acute enough to notice that it didn't rumble and squeak like Schaller's truck. There was a pause and then sounds of feet on the porch, a knock at the door. Hobe sat. Another sound . . . Schaller's truck coming, stopping in an unaccustomed place; Schaller's hard door-slam, his feet on the porch; sounds of talk. . . . And then they came and stopped, surprised to see him just sitting there.

The other one was a state policeman. His tree-trunk thighs, big gun, and all the leather and metal he wore filled the room. Beside him Schaller looked like a spindly ghost blowing in a windstorm, but his eyes still burned and could not be extinguished. The policeman was embarrassed by his own bigness and health in the dilapidated place. He sat down in the dusty front room and played with his hat. He doesn't like this, Hobe thought. He doesn't know what to say.

"Y'see, that old dog has been goin' around beggin' at the neighbors'," the policeman began. "They didn't know much about the man. Old man, kept to himself.

Dog was comin' back again and again—they thought somethin' might have happened to the old man, an' they called us——"

It got dark in front of Hobe. Schaller's eyes burning in the darkness were like wild animal eyes. Hobe had nothing but those eyes in the darkness, yet he knew exactly what Schaller was going to say. A true son. He was a true son and not unhappy. It was no use being unhappy. It was no use standing against a world with no light, where nothing was real but Schaller's burning eyes. He had, as he had never had before, perfect knowledge of where he was and what was going to happen. Schaller began to speak exactly as Hobe knew he would speak, and it gave a comfort, a peace almost as pure as that which they had known together on the high peak overlooking Koven's death.

"You come to the right place. We been waitin'. Here's the boy. This boy. This is the boy that done it."

Schaller was as enthusiastic as he had ever been— his eyes were bright, his gestures full of animation. When he had finished speaking, he looked satisfied. Hobe didn't mind. All during the morning the picture he had of Schaller and the picture he remembered of Koven had begun to merge in his mind; he couldn't tell them apart any more. Maybe Koven had never existed as a man, but was only Schaller's dream. Maybe he himself was a dream in Schaller's mind. If it was true, it was good. Schaller would soon wake up and end him. He smiled slightly. Through the muffling silence of his disinterest and exhaustion he began to hear the policeman arguing with his father.

"What reason would he have? . . . There was talk in town that *you* and him was . . . The boy here, he's just summer help. Like I say, it don't make sense. . . ."

After a while he went over to Hobe and bent down and Hobe could feel his big presence and smell his slightly meaty breath. "Snap out of it, boy. They's a man named Koven, a man on a farm. He's lyin' in front of his barn, half in, half out, with a ax buried in his head. Do you hear what I'm tellin' you?"

"Yes, sir." A voice without overtones—half a voice really.

He heard the leather belt complaining around the man's large waist. "Don't fool with me, boy."

"No, sir."

"Did you have anything to do with it?"

Hobe looked at the policeman's face for the first time. It wasn't a strong face like Schaller's. Nothing burned in it, neither pride nor anger. It was the kind of face you forgot. When his tormentors in school grew up, they would have faces like that. "I did it. I forget why," he said. "I just did it, that's all."

The policeman got up and his heaviness made him breathe hard doing it. He turned to Schaller. "He ain't one of them feeble-minded from up to the school, is he?"

"Nope"—with just the shadow of a smile—"not from the school. . . ."

"Well . . ." The policeman sounded like a housewife who had finished her ironing and was eager to put the things away. "We better be goin' into town. Mr. Schaller; you better come too. You got a friend to call —someone who can take care of your stock for you while you're—uh—away?"

That was when Schaller tried to race at Hobe, to strike him down and kill him for what he had done; but the policeman saw it and got him pinned before he reached Hobe, who hadn't moved. Schaller burst into tears.

"Now, come on," the policeman said, embarrassed. "Take it easy, now."

"He killed my neighbor! Koven was my neighbor. In the old times, people depended on their neighbors. Nowadays . . ."

The policeman dropped his hold and ordered Schaller out ahead of him. Then he had a big hand on Hobe's shoulder. Hobe felt his shoulder thin and small under that hand.

"What's your name, son?"

That word . . .!

Hobe looked up at the policemen. "You never think about a dog getting gray, do you? That dog had gray all around his muzzle." His hand had cupped a little into the shape that would hold the muzzle of the old dog. "A person couldn't figure on a thing like that, could he? . . . I mean he'd have to see it before he could know . . . that they get gray just like people . . ."

2   Children of Joy

THEY HADN'T CHANGED SINCE I had grown up. The only difference was the one that had always been there: the difference between what they were and the way they appeared in the family stories. My names for them had skipped the generation between. They were my great-aunts, really; Imah was called "Imah" by my mother and so by me, though she was my grandmother. Once, impossibly, the aunt across the table had been a flirtatious Hester, dance-mad and party-loving, who had spent a week's wages on ribbons and been beaten for it. She was a large, soft woman now, her hair white and scant.

Next to me, Aunt Ida was sniffing as she tossed a bad nut among the shells on the table. Whenever I saw her, she would enter something new into the catalogue of her illnesses: "conditions." I couldn't see or imagine the girl who had been arrested and jailed for inciting a mob to riot, and that at a time when women, especially immigrant women, did not command attention.

Imah herself must have been other things before she was my grandmother, but in 1890 people must have been different, born old, with only their bodies to age after that.

"I can feel the cold through the walls," Aunt Ida said.

Imah sighed. "I'll go turn up the thermostat."

"Thermostats don't make real heat." But Imah got up and went out of the kitchen and the aunts adjusted dutiful expressions on their faces.

"Enjoying your vacation?" Aunt Hester asked me.

"Yes. Before you came, Imah was telling me about the days in the old country, in Zoromin."

"A waste of time," Aunt Ida said. "Hitler chewed it up, but on its best day, in a good year, it wasn't anything to begin with."

I was shocked. "How can you say that when family life was so much closer, when the air was clean and the rivers and streams were unpolluted, when people ate natural foods and were so much richer spiritually than we are today?"

They looked at each other in what I could have sworn was confusion.

"I don't think they heard about all that in Zoromin," Aunt Hester said. "About the water—well, the women washed clothes in it, the horses drank, the tanner dumped into it. About clean water they didn't hear in Zoromin."

"At least things were what they seemed to be," I said. "You didn't look at everything through a plastic package. People, too. People were what they seemed to be, not packages with an 'image.' You didn't grow food for looks but for nourishment. People remember the old-fashioned cooking, and that's why."

"Oh, *that* cooking," Imah said, having come back and seated herself. She grinned and her hand went up to her mouth. Aunt Ida caught her eye and turned away, biting her lip. "Old-fashioned . . ." And then the three of them began to laugh.

I had gotten up to make more tea. I turned from the stove to look at them, chuckling comfortably above their bosoms.

"What's funny? What's the joke?"

They looked at me and laughed again, Aunt Ida checking the slipping wig she hadn't worn for years.

"You poor girl," Imah said. "You grew up in such a good home, you didn't have time to learn the simplest truths."

"It isn't her fault," and Aunt Ida wiped a crumb from her cheek. I came back to the table and began to clear a place among the nuts and shells. "Listen," Ida went on, and impaled my arm with a forefinger. "First is a family so poor that there is no piece of cloth without a hole. Our father traveled, following the breezes of other men's moving. He sent money in years that ended with two and seven. We saw him coming and going when the road bent that way or when business was bad. Of course, we had our own work, painting the lead soldiers. All of us. I thought you knew about that."

"Yes, but what does it have to do with cooking?"

She shook her head and clucked, then looked at me and shook her head again. "God help us! What has happened to the Jewish mind? There *was* no cooking, only hunger. We ate potatoes and weak soup, and if you're hungry enough, it's a banquet."

"But Uncle Reuben says——"

"Now there," Aunt Hester said, "walks a sage. To this day, if a thing doesn't give him heartburn, he thinks it wasn't worth eating."

Imah shook her head. "What cook can match herself against hunger and memory?"

Aunt Hester said, "We all carry a dream about Mama's chicken. If they set to music what we feel and remember of that chicken, Beethoven would be a forgotten article altogether."

Ida mused, "I think I know what chicken it was. It was the big one the Nachmansons gave us when they left to come to America."

"Tell me something," Imah asked. "What did it taste like, that chicken?"

"How should I know?" Hester shrugged. "We had to save it for Papa and the boys. By the time they finished, there wasn't anything left."

"I don't think I had any either," Ida said. "You see"—and she turned to me—"the chicken we didn't eat is the one we remember. That chicken is always tender."

"You're both ashamed to tell me," Imah insisted. "People took pieces of that chicken when it was still cooking."

"I didn't touch it." Hester said. "Not a shred."

Imah smiled. "Was I the only one? I thought maybe someone else did too. . . ."

"You little no-good, you! And Mama blamed Izzy!"

"Well, if you ate it, why did you ask what it tasted like?"

"Because I was so frightened, I just pushed it into my mouth and swallowed it and never tasted anything."

Ida asked, "If it was such a big chicken, how come there wasn't enough for us?"

"Wasn't there someone else?" Imah murmured. "I seem to remember——"

"My God, you're right!" Hester cried. "The Saint's children came!" Her eyes sparkled and she sat smiling over this lost moment found among all the million since.

"It was an honor, the Saint's children. We must have invited them to come and eat with us—it wasn't often we could invite someone for Shabbos dinner. That was why there wasn't enough. . . ."

Her eyes were full of warmth. She turned to me. "Our Saint was a wonderful man. We looked up to him, you have no idea; more than a scholar. People used to quote him like Torah. . . ." Then she waved at herself deprecatingly. "Such a man, and look how I forgot him. I wonder where his children are now."

"His name was Simcha," Imah explained to me. "It means joy. People used to call his sons 'The Children of Joy.' "

"What a crew!" Ida said. "They were boils on the backside of Zoromin. I wonder on what backside they are boils now?"

"Ida, how can you say such a thing!" Heads came up, Imah and Hester's mouths widening in unison.

"What did I spit on something holy, that you should look so stunned? Your Saint was a madman who starved his wife and beggared his children. If it's all the same to you, I won't waste clearing my throat to bless him."

"It isn't right to talk that way," Imah said, motioning toward me. "Your talk is only confusing. It's enough the Gentiles have stopped trying to tear down Judaism and left the job to Jews, who do it better."

Ida had her fire up. "Who said anything about Judaism? If that lunatic is Judaism, you can write me off the list—I'lll dip myself tomorrow." She sat back, cracking righteously. Shells and nutmeats showered from her hands.

"Aunt Ida thinks he was crazy," I said to Hester, who was sulking. "What makes you think he was a Saint?"

"I'll tell you," Aunt Hester said, "and afterwards, Ida can have her say. I'll tell you the facts and you can judge for yourself. Zoromin has nothing to be ashamed of, and neither do the Jewish people. There was, in our town, in Zoromin, a very pious and saintly man——"

"That's facts?" Ida crowed.

"I *said,* a very pious and saintly man. Origianlly, the family was well off—or as well off as anyone gets in a town like that. Anyway, Simcha was raised with a warm coat in winter and a full belly and good, dry shoes. . . ."

"What a pity his children weren't as well off as he. . . ."

"Ida. . . ."

"All right, go on."

"I don't know how it happened, but it was soon after he was married (a beautiful girl from a fine family. How she loved him and looked up to him!) Anyway, out of a clear sky, he came home one day, God-struck, changed. That day he gave away all his fine things, opened his house to the poor, and declared himself a refuge for anyone who was needy. During the day he walked miles, visiting the sick and hungry. Any penny extra went to the poor. He became even more pious than he had been before, and shamed many people who were more comfortable into being better Jews by his example.

"Well, his wife gave birth, and on each occasion he gave a party—not for the relatives, but for the poor, whose tongues didn't touch a piece of butter-cake from one year to the next. His Sabbaths were like the Sabbaths angels must have; his door was never closed.

"I remember most of all, his gentleness. The men in Zoromin worked like animals, sixteen, seventeen hours a day, in little shops, or walking to sell town to town, at the mercy of any robber or policeman on the way. Their lives and spirits became twisted because of it." She made a twisting motion with her old fingers.

"These men weren't gentle with their wives and they had no time to be loving to their children, or to say a pleasant word. What if they whipped a child by mistake and found it out later? They never apologized to that child or admitted the wrong, and if the child . . ."

Suddenly she was that child who had always been waiting for the incident to be found again, the anger and despair fresh although the cause had passed seventy years, and the father and the mistake and the town itself were no more. Weren't the old supposed to have forgiven everything long ago?

It frightened me a little. Maybe it frightened her too, because she turned from it quickly and hunted her thought again.

"It was no easy place, Zoromin, but there was one man there who would pick up a child who fell in the mud, and brush its clothes off and comfort it. There was one man who would notice if a woman's basket was too heavy and would help her.

"There were women, certain women, Ida, if you remember, who lived outside of town, and our people didn't count them as Jewish women, although we knew one of them was the cobbler's own cousin. These women had no one and nothing and our women spat at them in the streets. Simcha invited these women to his Sabbaths too; and when they were sick, he sent his own wife to nurse them. He used to say, 'The poor should not be denied the blessing of giving,' and he sent money to Jerusalem in their name."

While Hester talked, I looked at Imah and saw her following with an intense look, her lips moving slightly with the words.

"Did you know this Simcha?" I asked her.

"Yes, yes," she said a little vaguely. "I heard of him as a very good man, a very saintly man." She seemed to be listening and answering to something else.

Aunt Ida had been gathering in silence. "Well, don't worry about a place in heaven for that man," she said. "If there is a heaven, he's too good for it altogether; but for the Sages of Zoromin, he was just right. Can you imagine"—and she waved at Aunt Hester—"a grandmother there, and still an innocent. Hester, you don't know any more now than you did when you were ten.

"*He* was the Saint, that Simcha, and his family, who

weren't saints, were only cold hungry, and a burden on the town. Watch out for saints, Hester; they eat more than you think. When the saint decrees that his wealth be given to the poor, somebody has to stand baking all those little bread rolls that are given out of his great love. He says, 'Don't hand the beggar food at the door; ask him in, for is your brother.' Someone has to clean the cups and the table and the floor after the visit of a hundred brothers. Someone has to fill the house of hungry stomachs with the smell of baking bread. The saint's clothes are ragged, but he won't get new ones. Which is easier, I ask you—to darn a thread-bare coat or to make a new one? Someone has to fix and fix again that saintly garment, and draw the saint's frown when she curses old cloth that won't hold a needle!

"For heaven's sake, Hester, why do you think The Children of Joy were with us to eat that chicken? Reb Simcha knew he could be rich if he chose; he thought his children had the same choice he did. Those boys could hear a meat bone being dropped into soup half a mile away. If a man brushed a crumb from his beard, there was their knock on his door. . . . And why not? They were starving."

"What are you saying?" Hester looked scornfully at her sister. "That God should run to Zoromin to do the baking? The horror you speak of was that the saintly man drew his wife and children into his sanctity and caused them to do pious things——"

"Without the choice!" Ida cried.

"Aha!" Hester leaped up, her face glowing. Sixty of her years had fallen away, sixty pounds and all the chins and all the knotted veins that contended in her legs, and all the thousand compromises of a lifetime. "'Where did that leave them then? Why, with all the rest of Zoromin! Without a choice, hungry and cold, and wondering if the prayer has always to be drowned by the rumbling in the belly. *But . . ."* (My God, she *had* been beautiful! The old, brown family photographs had missed it all, standing her up dead like an apple in a fruit dish; but she had been dancing with all those bright ribbons, and it was more than the ribbons her father had beaten her for. It had been the headlong, headstrong, passionate eagerness he must have seen in her.)

"With our Simcha, they had a look, Ida, a little minute's venture into the way people should be, the way the holy books tell them to be. Those men, the ordinary men of Zoromin—to them the Torah was only rules, and they never asked why: Wear tefillin, or God will strike you. Don't blow out a candle on the Sabbath or God will cripple you. In that poor place we had a holy man walking, alive, to show the people that a man is not an animal, that there is more than hunger and rules for what is forbidden!"

"And the people saw glory in this one-man Eden, this walking paradise in Zoromin? They did not. They were smarter than you think, Hester. They knew that a poor man gives less charity than a rich one, and that Simcha's children should have been his charity. They weren't exalted, Hester, they laughed at him and despised his wife and children. Children of Joy was a bitter title; as bitter as Chosen People in those days. We were all Children of Joy in Zoromin, singing in the synagogue and starving."

"If the world knew virtue when it saw virtue, wouldn't *men* be Torah? Some didn't laugh at him, Ida. I didn't laugh. Didn't we have hard years after Zoromin? Didn't we need the memory of goodness? He was good, a saint."

"A madman. If Zoromin had been rich enough to build a madhouse, he would have had the master bedroom."

"A saint!"

"A madman!"

"Don't you see?" Imah cried at them as they stood tight-faced, shouting against each other. "He's only mad in English, not in Yiddish. He . . . The *English* makes him mad; in Yiddish he's still a saint!"

Their anger had overflowed their bodies, and suddenly, without reason, it found a home in me. I found myself grinding out words from a source I hadn't known was in me.

"What kind of people are you," I cried. "You had everything my friends and I admire, and you threw it away. You had all the security of the ceremonies and beliefs, lives full of meaning, dignity, and reality. That's what I came to Imah for, to find out how it was lost, the wonderful home life, when parents and children knew how to be loving and peaceful with one another; when there was the simple truth, not like today, all clouded and complicated. And now you've been so perverted by false values and materialism, you can't even remember what the old days were like!" Then, impossibly, "Haven't you any respect for your elders?!"

Dead silence. . . . Then a first, small edge of sound from Hester. The edge broke, and then the others came laughing in behind and in the end they conquered me and took me with them, defeated and captive in laughter.

"At least," Ida gasped, "she can still make Jewish jokes." We laughed till tears ran down our faces.

"Zoromin was a poor village," Ida wept. "Maybe they were too poor to afford a real saint."

"After all," Imah wept, "without some saint or other, what would people do?"

"I want saints," I wept, "but I want real ones."

"Who could afford it but Americans?" Hester was gasping. "Listen, when a woman can't have diamonds, she wears rhinestones; and when she can't have rhinestones, she wears glass and holds up her head."

"Is it true—did you mean it when you said that a man can be a saint in Yiddish and a madman in English?"

"If not," Imah said, and got up to get a Kleenex, "wouldn't we all be saints?"

"Then the dream of America was a fantasy—the hope was a lie!"

"American!" Aunt Hester said affectionately, and blew into her handkerchief. "Who would imagine, in so little time, our family would have such Americans?" She gazed at me with deep pride. "Look at her, she doesn't understand a single thing! . . . Oh, my knee aches so, I think I've been sitting in a draft!"

3   *The Lucero Requiem*

THE WEARY CHORUS WAS GOING over it again, and the four soloists waited in vain for their entrances. The music lacked form and rhythm, and the chorus' notes seemed to have been chosen at random. During a break, Harold Bropes, the tenor, leaned over to Max and whispered, "Where did they dig this thing up?"

"I don't know." Max shrugged. "I never heard of it."

"Somebody said the composer was a local bird, Spanish, Southern Colorado somewhere. Sponsor the minorities, but this is ridiculous!" Harold guffawed softly and flipped back the pages of his score. The thought crossed Max's mind that Harold hadn't exchanged so many words with him since rehearsals had begun and that dislike of the music was probably the only thing the four soloists would agree on.

The chorus stumbled again. Had work ever gone this badly? Max remembered times when he hadn't liked the music or the conductor or another singer, but usually an excitement came with the thought of performance, and there was a general camaraderie, even of despair, that overrode whatever else there was to complain about. He couldn't remember any other time when people just nodded good evening to one another and went home after a rehearsal. Joan Gideon, the soprano, was new and very young, worried, no doubt about her first big role, but Max had worked with Harold before and been friendly enough. Down the row was Abby Denicek, the contralto, with whom he'd worked more times than he could remember; yet from the beginning of these rehearsals there had been none of the usual joking between the soloists or among the chorus, and no horseplay. Perhaps it had something to do with the music itself. Maybe its formlessness and lack of continuity was being translated into a feeling of separateness and distance between the singers. He wondered if his own slight depression was a function of the music, like another set of overtones.

Max found himself sitting up after the rehearsal that night, studying the score. No wonder Halvard, the conductor, was getting disgusted. They were still unable to work out the transitions between chorus and solos. He flipped through his part impatiently. It wasn't the first night he had taken the score to bed with him and tried to see intelligibly somewhere. Who in hell was Naçencio Lucero? He wasn't one of the new young Denver composers, or one of the old ones, and he wasn't connected with the University. What had gotten the Music Department interested? It was probably, as Harold had said, someone pushing the idea for the novelty of a premier performance.

At the next rehearsal Max went out to the campus early and stopped in at the library to look in Rollinder's *Musicians' Supplement*. There it was:

Lucero, Naçencio: 1923–1943
Born Blanca, Colo. Choral setting of Pueblo rain prayer, 1940.
Strong Spanish-Indian influence. Served U.S. Infan-

try WW II. Three choral works: *Missa Azteca, Missa Kiva, Native Requiem* for 4 Voices and Chorus. Mss. bequeathed to Music Department Univ. Colo. Died Italy, Aug. 16, 1943. 7 compositions extant. *Missa Azteca* performed Vienna Academichor 1952, Harvard-Radcliffe Chorale 1960.

Not much help there. Max went on to rehearsal dutifully and did his best, but he was still irritated with the music and the people who were working with him. The only joy was in listening to Joan sing.

She was young, arrogant, and too impatient to spend much time with phrasing or interpretation, but it didn't seem to matter. She covered octaves as easily as single steps—never straining for a note or ending short of breath. Her ease was thrilling; her voice had abundance, certainty, and strength; and no tedious compromises. Max was a good musician and he knew it. The pleasure he got from listening to her made him a little confused; the vocal shading was poor, the phrasing rudimentary, yet . . .

Rehearsal was over; he sighed and closed his score. Whatever musicianship Joan learned, it wouldn't be from this.

The next rehearsal was no better, although Max had practiced his part with bitter determination. When the session was over, he nodded absentmindedly to Halvard and the others and began his elaborate preparations for going out into the icy night. He had minded all this a great deal when he was younger—the muffler, hat, and the scarf to protect his chest, throat, and ears. It had made him feel pampered and sissified, such elaborate care of his body, such concern over the right foods, the breathing, the exercises. He had tried to equate this with the fuss orchestral musicians made over their instruments, protecting them from shock and temperature changes. Now this care had become habit and he dressed slowly.

When he was ready, he saw with no particular surprise that everyone else had gone. Pushing out into the foyer of the auditorium, he met Abby adjusting the funny fur cap she often wore.

"Cold night," he said and smiled. He liked Abby. Her contralto voice wasn't powerful, but it was rich and well placed and she used it intelligently. Over the years he had come to value her knowledge, her musicianship, and her opinion on points of style. It occurred to him that after the first few rehearsals she had stopped waiting for him so they could walk to the parking lot together, picking over the work or talking shop. It bothered him that he hadn't noticed this before, and he suddenly found himself shy with her. "Uh—you going to the car?"

"Yes," she said smiling. "I think so."

They laughed, and he relaxed. "What's wrong, Abby? What's wrong with the four of us?"

They had come out into the night and the cold air shocked them. Max was so bundled up that he had to turn his whole body in order to look at her. She was facing straight ahead, impassively, as though she hadn't heard him.

"You must have felt this too," he said, "unless it's all in my mind, but I can't figure out why I feel so— so damn lonely. I don't like the music, but it's not the first time. I've sung with Halvard before; he's no George Szell, but he's competent. Harold is okay; you're fine; Joan is weak on experience, but she sings like an angel. Why is there this—this deadness among the four of us? We're jarring; the voices don't blend; and when we sing those damn trios and quartets, it's as though we're singing against one another. After rehearsal everybody scowls good night and goes home."

"Can't you figure it out?" she asked. He thought he heard bitterness in her voice.

"No. The only singing around here is Joan's."

"Joan is a bitch," Abby said quietly; "a petty, opportunistic, self-centered bitch."

Max was shocked and then embarrassed at the rawness of her hatred. "Let's see . . . you're trying to tell me something. . . ."

But she didn't laugh and Max cropped his bantering tone. "Abby, I've never seen you so violent about anyone. I don't know what's going on between you two, but it may be part of what's ruining everything for all of us. I mean, besides the music."

"We sing as if each of us was singing alone, but we sing duets too, Max. What about the duets—yours and mine?" Her voice sounded tight, but whether from the cold or not, he didn't know.

"Well?"

"Well nothing. We're gracious with each other. . . . Don't laugh—it's the word I mean. We play to the lead phrases in each other's part. In the *Sanctus,* you throw me that D flat and then you sing quietly so that I can echo it two bars later. And sometimes I pull up quickly so you can get a good running start when you need the power."

"That kind of thing takes years of experience, working together, knowing the music. This is Joan's first big role. She has four solos, as many duets and trios; it's the equal of a starring role in an opera. She's brand-new. Give her a chance."

"I can't," Abby insisted. She was sounding a bit shrill, not bothering to protect her voice. "She won't let me. Max, have you ever been cut off a half-second before your note ended? It's like coming down flat-footed. It makes you sound bad and the one who pulls the stunt gets off scot-free. She and I have a dozen spots that are natural for echo and re-echo, but when

her voice is supposed to fade a little, playing to my part, she rides over me like the Roman army. I've tried again and again and it's always the same." They had reached the parking lot and for a minute she hesitated. He knew she was embarrassed. She had sounded malicious and bitter, but she was also dead serious. "I know, Max, she's very affecting and very young, and I'm jealous of her voice." She smiled at him. "Why should that surprise you? I may be middle-aged, but I'm not deaf."

"I'm sorry," he said. "I guess I didn't think you knew it. I've been jealous often enough, but I never had the guts to say so."

"She's a shark," Abby said quietly. She had gotten into her car. She closed the door and they waved good night through the window. As Max pulled away in his own car, he saw Abby still fumbling in her purse for her keys.

Leaving the lot, he turned left, off campus, and half-unconsciously a melody started to grow in his mind and free itself. He turned the car out onto the highway, a long, straight stretch, deserted at this time of the night. He was doing seventy and the motor was giving him a C sharp. He was suddenly aware that the music in his mind was one of his solos, one he hadn't practiced for weeks. As he followed it, it began to rise in him until it burst from his throat, full voice. He drove through the darkness singing, the melody wheeling and turning at the top of his range like a huge, primeval bird that circles and, in syncopated beats, follows over a hundred hills and valleys the invisible contours of the air.

Max waited excitedly for the next rehearsal. The single bit of music had rooted itself in him and now it wouldn't let him go. At work, he found himself humming it, dipping and sliding joyfully over his notes;

feeling a rhythm, a pattern he had never heard before. Maybe there were more secrets hidden in the music, waiting for him. When he sat down in his chair at rehearsal and opened the score, it was with an excitment he hadn't felt since the work began.

Halvard started with the chorus. Max listened intently, trying to hear what he had heard in his solo. It wasn't there. The voices still sounded hollow and disconnected. The choral part led into Joan's solo and, with Abby's words in his mind, he found himself listening under the brilliance and being bothered by something more than faulty phrasing and flashiness. Studying the score, he followed as Joan began a duet with Harold. At each entrance and release, she was hanging on her best notes a fraction of a second overtime, putting Harold off his entrances and taking his releases before he finished them. When she trilled over his voice, she drew too much attention to the ease of her performance, singing about the fires of hell in a bright, almost operetta style. And she was magnificent. Her youth and talent somehow made the excesses work. There she hung happily, like a kid balanced on a fence, showing off, delighting in the danger. When Harold took up what should have been the major voice, she didn't relinquish the lead, and all Max could think was: God, is he outclassed!

Luckily for Harold, he didn't realize how consistently he was being overreached. When the duet ended, he turned and grinned at Joan. She hesitated for a moment and then gave him a dazzling smile. Max could have sworn there was nothing arch or cynical about the smile; it was a look of pure happiness, and the whole bass section of the chorus which had seen it break over Harold in his fool's paradise, was warmed. Most people hearing the subtle contest lost and lost again by the tenor would simply conclude that he had a second-rate voice. Even then, Max couldn't agree

with Abby all the way. Joan was young and inex-
perienced and full of the newness and wonder of her
gift. Who could blame her for wanting so much?

The chorus hit flat behind him, and Halvard stopped
them and turned to the soloists. "I'll have to work this
part out from the beginning," he said, "You might as
well take the rest of the evening." They gathered their
things and began to leave the stage.

The thing to do, Max knew, was to take everyone
out for a beer. A few laughs would reduce the tension.
They had to sing together; they might as well start
trying to get through the performance in a decent way.
He wanted to say the words easily and casually, but
suddenly he found he couldn't. He didn't really want to
go out for beer; he wanted to go to the back of the
auditorium and listen to the chorus. Standing away from
it, he might be able to hear in the blend of voices some
pattern that was eluding him. It was a rare chance; he
might not have another.

"Joan"—he caught up to her, still undecided what
to say, and then he blurted—"let's go back and listen."

She smiled at him, flattered a little by the attention.
"You're a glutton for punishment." They were offstage
and at the word "punishment," Abby and Harold
turned, caught by the word. Joan gave a little shrug of
disinterest. "There's nothing until the *Lacrymosa*."

Abby smiled coldly, a smile that showed how intense
her hatred was. "Music is made," she said, "even when
you are not singing."

"Really?" Joan laughed as though she had said something witty. Then she turned and pretended to be listening to the chorus. "They're flat again. Ugh!"

Harold had suddenly put his knuckles to his mouth.
"I just realized—we have to sing this in two weeks!"

For a moment they all stood shocked, counting off
days. The chorus went flat again and they looked at one
another grimly. The hundred and fifty voices could not

be dismissed as mere background anymore. Like a precocious and unpredictable child due to appear in company, its moods were suddenly a source of dread. They listened in silence and then, one by one, slipped away and went home. No one said good night.

Now everyone realized how close the time was. Rehearsal nights were doubled. Halvard began to pick and quibble and make the chorus repeat phrase after faulty phrase. After rehearsals they looked keelhauled, the soloists grim and strained. Harold began to wear loud ties; he got jauntier in an irritating way. Joan seemed more brittle; Abby more rigid and pedantic; and Max found it harder and harder to concentrate. He couldn't figure out whether the heaviness he felt was fear of a bad performance or disgust at the childish conflict among the four of them. They tested one another, giving and taking little vindictive remarks with strangely avid pleasure, and the more Max tried to help, the more he blundered. Once, after Abby made a crack about the arrogance of young singers, he had tried to lighten it, saying that Joan was naturally proud of being young. He had spoken carelessly, quickly, to ease the moment, but it was a tacit acknowledgment that Abby's remark was correct, and it had earned him a place in the war from which he couldn't step without creating rancor on both sides. Harold had also been drawn in, on Joan's side, and they all faced the last rehearsals and the concert itself in a grim tension, hiding behind the pages of their scores and riding out angrily on the staff lines that carried their music.

Max was more and more taken with that music. It began to echo in him against the rhythm of his steps—a beat, beat, then a dropped-beat-upbeat, one-two, da-da-*dum*. He had had to make peace with the dissonances and hollow intervals in his part, and now he was becoming used to them and to a new kind of order in what he sang.

But the choral parts wouldn't come. On Wednesday night Max asked Halvard if he could take a break and go back in the auditorium. "Who will sing your part?" Halvard asked.

"I could sing it from there."

Halvard looked disgusted. "Do you want to hear the balance or just get away from whatever is going on among the four of you?"

Max was surprised. He hadn't realized that the coldness of their performance had been so noticeable. How foolish to imagine that it hadn't! He was about to say something, but Halvard was gesturing him to go back.

The chorus began, as Max walked down the aisle singing at half-voice the random, staccato notes that were written for him. He didn't like this section and even now had to fight a tendency to burlesque his part. As he went, he softened his voice and softened again in order to listen. The sounds had begun to blend and merge. They were doing the *Dies Irae,* chorus and solo voices singing of the souls of the dead rising for judgment, and from the bare, cavernous intervals, Max heard, like a vast echo, what seemed to be numberless, pinpoint-separate voices rising to whimper, gibber, plead, and harangue at the Gates of Heaven. As the other solo voices came and went in the clamor, he could hear that Joan and Harold were putting their sounds by rote, without phrasing.

"Sing scared," he muttered; "it's Judgment Day."

When the section was over, Halvard turned to Max, who walked back to the group. They were waiting for his word; only he had heard what an audience would hear. He shrugged and then looked up at the stage. "It's beautiful!"

The chorus, tense with exhaustion and ready for betrayal, broke into relieved laughter, and Max laughed too. "It does fit—really. The voices come out in those little staccato passages like little cries. . . ." The three other soloists were looking at Max with tolerant amusement. "You—you'll just have to hear it yourselves."

So they went back, one by one, dutifully, to "hear" and when they returned, nodded dutifully at Halvard. Abby gave Max a quick smile as she stepped past him and back into her place, but it was for encouragement, not agreement. She had liked his joy, not the music.

That night as Max lay somnolent in his bath, he listened to the music again. His mind began a daydream of the words of it. There were the Souls of the Dead; as far as the eye could see, old people, babies, parents, children, warriors, lovers, rising naked for the Last Judgment. None had yet been through the purifying fire; all were wearing their arguments and reasons and sins and glories tangled around them. Victims were crying for justice, villains for justification; the humble were begging, the arrogant demanding. Lovers were . . . He sprang out of the tub and ran to the phone, leaving a trail of water and dripping large drops on the phone book as he looked up Abby's number. Her husband, Frank, answered, and by the time she came to the phone, Max was feeling sheepish and irritated with himself.

"Hello?" It was obvious that his call had wakened her.

"Hello, Abby. This is Max. Uh—do you know the bit we do right in the middle of the *Dies Irae?*"

"What is it?" she said sleepily.

"I just figured it out, the staccato notes there . . ."

"That's good, Max," she said vaguely, and yawned. "Well, good night, then." And she hung up.

They tried it at the next rehearsal, as Max had heard it in his mind. Abby had listened to his idea, shrugged,

and said, "Why not?" So when his voice rose against
hers, he bit off the ends of the notes and she answered
as he had suggested, stridently, in a hard, almost tone-
less series of ascending cries. Up and up they went,
louder and shriller. They began to sound like
squabbling lovers, each blaming the other and shouting
his innocence before the Judge of the Last Day. Behind
them the chorus began to get the idea; it wailed and
stung and here and there the single voices of gifted ones
broke as if by force from the mass of sound to cry and
be swallowed up again. The pitch rose. They could
see Halvard looking at them, smiling. They went louder and more strident until they couldn't contain their
joy and both Abby and Max burst out laughing, the
chorus petering out behind them.

"Good God!" Halvard said into their dying sound.
"Of course! of course!"

Then, everyone laughed, the first spontaneous and
healing sound Max had heard since rehearsals had
started; but as he looked around, he noticed that Joan
seemed puzzled, and later, when he asked her how she
liked their interpretation, she said, "I can't understand
how Abby could fall for such a trick—making her
voice sound ugly on purpose. You sounded good,
though." There was no use trying to explain.

There were only two more rehearsals before the
concert. Max could feel fear in the chorus and an awful tension in Halvard. He knew he had to talk to
Abby, to work for some kind of unity in the week left.
So he called her. "Let me take you to dinner. We could
'dine out' at that three-two beer place off campus and
then go to rehearsal."

"Sounds great," she said. "I'll wear my beanie."

It wasn't great. The jukebox was so loud they
couldn't talk without shouting, and they were afraid

of the strain on their voices. In the end they talked in the pauses between paroxysms of amplified Rock.

"You know, we should *all* be here," Abby said, "drinking, talking, and dropping names."

Max glared at the jukebox. "We should all be somewhere where we could work it out. . . . Are you scared?"

"Yes." She nodded. "Every year a dozen singing groups spin Bach and Haydn in their graves, but that music is familiar; people know how it's supposed to sound. The mind corrects a sour note or a wooden baritone. I don't like this music as much as you do; but if we kill it now, we may be killing it outright and forever, and that isn't fair. If only that bitch——"

"Cut it out," he said. The jukebox stopped her. Afterward: "Look, I don't want to talk about you and Joan, but about the music. Last month I didn't like it either and now I wonder how I could have been so deaf to it. I think you could learn to like it too, but there just isn't time."

"Well, what *is* there time for? If you talk about the work, you'll have to talk about Joan. She's out to kill me. I tried to help and then I tried to leave her alone. What else is there?"

Jukebox again. They waited.

"One more thing." Max softened his tone so that the words might shock her less. "There is one more thing to try and that is to give in, to let her have it all her way."

"Do you know what she wants?" Abby said with quiet fury. "She wants all her singing to be solo; duets and trios just provide her with a muted undertone, a harmony."

The jukebox again. Again they waited.

"All right. Why don't we give in? You and I still have our parts. Last night I counted seven—no nine —sections where she doesn't sing at all. We can do whatever we want in those, and when Joan sings, we'll pull back and let her have it all to herself. How about it?"

"You say you like the music, yet you want it unbalanced that way?"

"If it has to be," he said grimly. "I have a feeling Lucero didn't write it for people like us to sing, but for people like her. The temperament wouldn't matter to him because she's brilliant enough."

"Then music is for showmen, not musicians."

The jukebox again. . . . The food came. They ate angrily and then left, finding it easier to talk as they strolled toward the campus.

Max realized that he would have to put the situation personally, as it had come to him. He said, "You know, when I was Harold's age, I was sure I could be great if only the conductor was right and the roles were right. If I didn't get famous, or wasn't given top roles, it was because my voice wasn't being brought out correctly. It hurt for a while. I saw plots, intrigues; but somewhere along the line I found I had begun to listen to the music for its own sake. I was like a man marrying for money and then falling in love with his wife. I began to yearn to belong to a career I already had. I started working very hard because I wanted knowledge to bring me greatness. It didn't. It brought me competence. I'm grateful for that, but suddenly, greatness—a greater talent than mine—comes along, and I find I have to shut up and get out of the way."

"Max, your voice is better than mine, and God knows, hers is. Lots of people's voices are. But I always thought that at least my musicianship made up for a lot I didn't have. Now you're saying it doesn't— that it has no value."

"Who said it has no value? How many great ones are there? If the Bach and the Lucero are going to get sung, our kind are going to have to do nine tenths of the singing because there aren't enough top musicians with great voices to go around."

"Is that *all?*"

"Well," he said, and found himself grinning, "maybe it's not *all*. We get to listen to them, to learn."

"And do what, when they make our duets solos, when they ride us down?"

"Wear the wheel marks and try to smile."

"Oh, *thanks.*"

The campus was full of young people out in the unseasonably mild night.

"I feel like Methusaleh's mother," Abby said disgustedly. "Methusaleh's mother with wheel marks."

Max laughed.

"Max, I just remembered the first time I ever saw you. Good Lord, fifteen years ago. . . ."

"You thought: There goes one hell of a handsome fellow!"

"Not exactly. It was an audition for the Beethoven, *Missa Solemnis*. Frank and I had just moved here and I didn't know anybody. They were holding the audition at some church, I remember. I went early; you were standing in a corner singing the *Confutatis Maledictis* —up to your neck in contrition, remorse, stench of sin—and grinning from ear to ear."

"I like to sing," he said sheepishly.

She smiled in the dying light. "You do, don't you?"

He nodded.

"Okay," she said. "You win."

The singing had a quality of panic to it. They had all suddenly become aware of how close the performance was. Halvard, usually placid, raged and barked, and the chorus shifted nervously while he scolded them, sighing over repeated stops for correction.

During the second hour they took the whole work straight through for the first time. With the experience of perfected parts, the members of the chorus found that they were beginning, slowly, to understand the whole. They were on key, moving toward a vague but present form in the work, and they were rewarded with a humble amazement at their own power to move.

In the *Domine Jesu,* the bass section felt for the thunder it was meant to produce—and found it. The tenors took their cue, Halvard crying, "Fine!" Altos and sopranos followed. The upper voices blew into a gale, "Deliver us," the basses rumbled, "from the Lion's mouth. . . ." Then unison built—forte, fortissimo—and suddenly all the voices exploded in desperate joy—the *Sanctus.*

At the end of the choral part some of the singers were in tears; and the conductor, sweating and exultant. "Now!" he cried, over the sound he dared not break, "tempo will increase, sound diminish. Until the soloists come in. Keep it taut . . . taut." And he cued the soloists, who began fortissimo, as Max had once said scornfully, like four five-hundred-pound angels shot out of cannon.

The chorus gradually stilled; the quartet faded as if those angels were beating in unison, slowing as they rose higher and still higher.

Max heard Joan beside him, too loud. She wasn't following the mood. Halvard waved her down slightly, but didn't want to stop. The sound seemed off, somehow, but the four went higher and softer still, until they had merged into a single beam of sound that slowly faded and was gone.

There was dead silence; a spontaneous, breath-caught gasp of awe. And in the silence, Abby's voice, a stage whisper. It had been pitched loud enough to be heard above talk and rustling scores; in the silence, it filled the room. Abby was leaning over to Joan helpfully, and whispering, "You were singing B-Flat there. It should have been A-Flat."

The room burst into uncontrollable laughter. Joan surely knew it was release from the tremendous power of the music that made them laugh so wildly, but her face went stiff with rage. Abby tried an apology, but there was really nothing to say.

The rehearsal continued and when it was over, Joan left immediately. The rest of the singers stayed on, not wanting to leave a place where they had been surprised in the act of creation. When they did go, they were quiet. No one wanted to disturb the sounds that hung shimmering in his mind.

Max saw Abby to her car. Looking out at him she said, "I wasn't trying to . . . I didn't mean . . . I was trying to *help*."

"I know," he said. "Don't worry about it."

By dress rehearsal, Max hoped that the moment would be lost in everyone's excitement at the music. He knew Joan wouldn't forget, but a good rehearsal could put the embarrassment in perspective.

Joan came late and sang her part looking straight ahead. Whenever the others worked with her, they gave ground; Abby so much that Halvard had to keep motioning her up, and afterward, spoke to her about it. "I don't want to keep pulling the sound from you."

Abby apologized and said she would work harder. Joan watched them from her place and then left quickly.

On Sunday afternoon Max dressed carefully in formal clothes. He wore a thick undershirt beneath the starched dickey because he sweated heavily when he did a concert. Before he left for the auditorium, he swallowed the tablespoonful of honey dictated by custom (energy, memory, richness in the tone). With all his years of performing, he was still nervous before he sang and wanted no one around him but other singers. When he got to the auditorium, he went backstage and sat down among the knots of nervous chorus members who were trying to chatter away their fear. Someone mentioned Abby's immortal comment to Joan at rehearsal, and the group laughed. Max looked around quickly to see if either of the women were there to hear it. They weren't, and he was relieved.

By the time all the soloists had arrived, it was only fifteen minutes to performance; time to go downstairs and warm up. They went quickly and no one spoke. Max remembered having done the Beethoven *Solemnis* more than once in a cascade of practical jokes, the Verdi *Requiem* with a roaring joy that took the soloists a mile past the beer joint one night, arm in arm, singing the *Hostias* at the tops of their lungs. Even when conductors were tough and temperamental, which this one wasn't. . . . He shrugged and began to get ready. He took several deep breaths and let them out slowly and then began a series of vocal eases, starting softly and never opening to full voice. He sang slowly, listening with care, testing the balance and richness of his tone. He was in good voice today; the fact was clinically objective but reviving, and it caused him to smile so that he went a little sharp.

When it was time, he picked up his score and started back upstairs. The chorus was already arranged onstage. He saw Joan waiting in the wings, worrying her hair over her finger. He went to her smiling. "Ready?"

She turned toward him, coolly professional: "Of course."

He didn't know what to say. He had always left the wings for battle, giving and taking a quip or an insult to break the tension, but even in her first solo performance, Joan wanted nothing from him. They stood together in silence until Halvard walked onstage from the other side. Abby and Harold came up, and the four of them went, one after the other, into the glare and the sound of applause.

Halvard called the chorus' attention with his eyes; he smiled at the four soloists, and then, putting his hands wide for the choral entrance, mouthed to them all, "Sing like hell." His hands cut down; the music began.

It went quickly. The entrance was hesitant, but soon the chorus forgot itself in the music. By *Te Decet Hymnus,* the singers had hit their stride, a wild, happy, syncopated roar of sound in which the soloists found themselves carried to their quartet by sheer momentum. There they took breath to dig in and work. Max and Abby haggled and nagged in their duet and fed each solo as lovingly as they could to bring out the subtle currents of the music. Solos and combined voices wove into choral parts—they were going to make it. Abby was letting Joan have her way, all of it; Joan was singing wide open, overriding everyone's part and punishing Abby until it seemed she had been reduced to an echo. Max knew the audience wasn't familiar with the music and probably wouldn't know the difference. They were going to make it solidly. The difficult parts were almost all behind them. The chorus was at *Libera Eas,* thundering and confident and exactly on pitch. From their tidal sea of sound the quartet rose again to its hushed single note, then the *Agnus Dei,* and *Lux Eterna.*

As Max sang, he heard his own voice filling the hall. There was a depth and timbre in it he had never known he could produce. Cadence by cadence he opened. All the power he needed was there at his will, his restraint of it, an almost palpable delight. He knew he had perfect command of breath, tone, range. For these few moments he felt himself working at height, and it was this music which had given him his glory. He was full of joy and gratitude. When it was finished, he turned, slightly in awe of what he had been allowed to do, to share it with the others.

He saw that Joan had stepped back and was bringing her score up to close away the audience. Then she turned toward Abby with a look of withering hatred. The chorus missed it; Halvard, busy with their entrance, missed it, and Max was left standing alone and helpless, his mind repeating stupidly: But we're almost through . . . we're almost through.

Halvard gave them a cue, Joan's score down, the entrances were made and the beat moved them on. Abby began, Joan followed. The first four bars were past, the second. Then, minutely and relentlessly, Joan sharped her pitch and began to sing louder, making Abby's voice seem heavy and flat. For a moment Abby looked puzzled, standing in her place and producing sounds that were without depth or tone. Then her eyes went to Joan. She shook her head once, looking straight at the soprano and singing the flat-sounding sequence.

When Max's entrance came, he moved in loudly, hoping to pull them both back, but Joan had edged her voice like a razor. It was too late to restore tonality. No one would believe the pitch that Abby was singing as she resisted Joan's almost irresistible power. Max's cadence ended and the warring duet swept on relentlessly toward its end in the choral fugue. With one last agonizing syllable, Abby sounded her A-Flat true, but beside Joan's sharped, brilliant voice it sounded like a mistake, tinny and off-tone. The full chorus overrode it and, pitching itself from the soprano note, turned into the final fugue a whole tone sharp. Halvard scowled, then winced, his left hand trying to fan them down.

As the fugue went on, the chorus realized that something was wrong—it was going too high. Some tried vainly to correct while others, pushed to the limits of their vocal ranges, shrieked falsetto notes to the marooned conductor. There was no reality, no up or down, only waves of sound on which they choked and groaned, breasting again to look for some marker in that ocean of mad tides. Abby, exhausted, hopeless and on pitch, gave a dozen dull-sounding cues, until Max himself began to wish she would give in.

After an endless passage without laws or boundaries, the fugue was over and the chorus stood shaken. There was no more for the vanquished contralto to do. She had ended her performance sounding old, and her look of cornered bitterness was a look of old age. Beside her, radiant and vivid, stood the soprano, her last notes triumphant. Max and Harold had a small linking part, unison, in support of the final choral *Requiem Aeternam*. It was a ringing statement, an affirmation of life in the presence of death. The four soloists stood still as it sounded past them, the power of it vibrating the floor beneath their feet. When the last note died, there was a silent moment of awe and then the audience broke with applause.

They were leaving. A ripped score, a dozen wads of Kleenex, and someone's forgotten raincoat were scattered in the dressing room. Most of the singers had gone home. Max was about to leave too when he saw Abby sitting very quietly just outside the dressing room in the little alcove where the stage lights were controlled. The chorus members must have trooped by her, still keyed up with the music and the excitement, leaving her in the little hollowness of their departure. He felt her exhaustion and had to warn himself against treating her like an invalid. Pity would give a reason to what Joan had done. "Hi," he said, "want a ride home?"

"My car's outside," she answered absently. "Frank worked today, thank God."

"Leave the car. My sister is making lasagne. Come on. We can get the car later." She looked so much a victim that he found himself getting annoyed. "Oh, Abby, come on. Not everybody fell for that trick—it isn't the first time a career got launched with a foot in someone else's face."

"So much," she said bitterly, "for competence."

Max began to feel tired; he always did after a concert. And he couldn't ask her if she had heard what he had done—he incredible thing he had done. "Come on," he said. "We'll eat and get plastered and plan revenge."

"I'd like to dedicate my first drink," she said quietly, "to Mr. Lucero. He writes a beautiful score. Why did I take so long to realize it? I knew I wasn't a great singer, but I thought I was a good musician. Imagine— to be in music for so many years and not be able to feel that strength or hear that beauty until you'd sung the thing fifty times. I'd like to write him a letter of apology, but I don't know where he lives. Who is he? Is he still writing?"

"He has three compositions for chorus and soloists. He died in World War II, in Italy."

"One of my generation after all," she said, and smiled. "Now I'll have to have that drink to the War Dead, although he isn't through being a casualty. Imagine having to depend on people like Joan, and people like me."

"To Immortals!" Max said, raising his arm, "who have to take their lumps forever."

"To a voice"—and Abby smiled—"whose lousy, crummy, vindictive, sharped-up note can sound so true that a chorus of a hundred and fifty people follows its lead——"

"To Competence!" Max shouted and gave a Bronx cheer.

"To A-Flat!" Abby howled.

"To Muzak!" Max cried.

"To Muzak!" she shouted after him, and, remembering the phrasing of something they had done together, she whispered the echo, "To Muzak!" Then a three-beat rest *In excelsis!*

4 Summer People

ON THE WAY, WE TALKED about Solon, and I told Ken and Chris more than I ever had before. When Ken and I were courting, we had shared the usual hometown memories, but less about the towns of our growing than about ourselves growing. When Chris was little, he had taken great delight in my reminiscences—school; Christmas; the ID bracelet I took from Peregoy's store and then had to take back; my best friend, Alice. When Ken and later Chris asked me why I'd left, I told them that Solon was small, too small for most of its young people, or for anyone who didn't want to be a farmer or a fisherman, or be married to one. I didn't tell them why *I* had left.

They knew that Aunt Louise had moved into the family home afterwards and had stayed on after my father's death and my mother's remarriage. Aunt Louise had died in May, Mother was needed elsewhere, and the cousins had written asking me to come to Solon and sort through the family things before the house was sold. I had put it off; but, late in June, Ken found he was free, Chris was out of school, and suddenly all of us were going, a vacation, they said, and there was no reason I could give against it.

We went by car, traveling slowly north and east, coming day after day closer to Solon and the sea. Between the cities the land began to change: on the highways a different texture and color to the banked earth shoulders; the foliage thicker and more varied; the air heavier, weighed with moisture and the scents of flowers that didn't grow back home. Still farther north and the rhythms of hills and ridges became powerfully familiar, and then the names of towns—Burdick, Towanda, Oak Gap. In spite of myself I felt a sharp, old excitement: "There's Solon Landing, over the hill. Keep right, Ken, let's go by the sea road."

A mile from Solon Landing, I made them get out and with ridiculous formality, introduced them to the Atlantic Ocean. Chris, no boy for The Gesture, spent the rest of the mile hunched down in his place, hoping nobody had seen us. Then, past a hundred landmarks no one knew, to Solon Landing. Things were the same. . . . Things were different. . . .

It was still June, but the Summer People had already begun. I'd forgotten about Summer People. They weren't really a part of Solon or of the Landing. I'd given my memories without them—describing the small harbor; the wharf, deserted in the daytime except for Charlie Yatikay, who seemed never to be anywhere else; the wharf street with its few supply stores; Peregoy's Post Office and General Store; and the road up from the harbor and over the hill to Solon itself, where most of the Landing people lived. My husband and son looked quizzically at me when we pulled into the Landing and found it full of color and people. Peregoy's hadn't changed and the buildings on the wharf were the same, but the dunes were full of sunbathers and umbrellas, the wharf street full of young people with transistor radios, and there were kids swimming off the mussel pier.

"Hey, Ma, I thought you said this place was dead." Chris had lately developed a way of turning what I said into statements with which I had to argue.

"I didn't say it was dead; I said it was quiet. Those are tourists—Summer People. In my day we never had them until after the Fourth of July."

Ken pulled the car up and said they would wait while I went in to Peregoy's to check for messages and mail.

The store was dark and cool; not a thing seemed changed. I went to the grocery section and looked down the row of shelves to see who was at the counter. It was Old Man Peregoy himself, looking no older. I got a few things for dinner and went to the counter. He began to ring them up automatically, without looking at me.

". . . and a half-gallon of milk, Mr. Peregoy, please. . . . Are there any messages for us?"

He did look then, annoyance familiar on his face. A moment and then the scowl broke to a smile, and behind me I could hear a slight shifting, well-bred surprise among the shoppers.

"Why—why it's John Clitheroe's girl, isn't it?" and his strong, dry hand came forward to shake mine. "You favor John more, now you've grown." He remembered "We were all sad when your aunt passed on; she was a fine woman. I suppose you've come to see to the house——"

"There isn't much to do," I said. "I have my husband and boy with me. Our name is Satterfield."

"Well, it's good to see you. I'll tell folks you're back. Staying long?"

"We can't stay long, but I did want my husband and son to see Solon." Which was a lie.

Mr. Peregoy was gossiping busily away, and every now and then I could look out of the corner of my eye and catch curious glances from the strangers moving among the racks of color film and sunglasses near the counter.

"I remember you as a youngster clearer than I do many of others," he was saying. "You used to run with those kids over to the Cove, didn't you? Barrientos—Alice, wasn't it?"

"Yes."

"Well, you know, most of those Portugees that lived over that way picked up and went. Never did have much to keep them. But that Alice married Charlie Conyers, and they live up to Conyers' there—three kids, just as dark as their ma. . . ."

My best friend, Alice—from the time we'd sat together in first grade needing to go to the bathroom and afraid to ask. Together we had fought the local feeling (we called it prejudice then) against "the Portugees." Watching the recent news, those struggles seem laughable; the arguments miniature, antique, and muted; but then, the fact of our friendship was lit with a kind of drama, and punctuated by the town's raised eyebrows. In the end there was still warmth between the two of us, even after the thing that separated me from Solon—after the bad things happened.

Mr. Peregoy was talking about the old ball teams. I thanked him and promised I would stop in with Ken and Chris. I left in the aura of his smile, pleased—though I laughed at myself—with the wistful desire I saw in the faces of the Summer People to be greeted as I had been.

Ken and I went through the old house before dark and I got up a light dinner on paper plates. Aunt Louise had seen death coming and had made it her last point of pride not to be caught unready. The dishes, bed-clothes, garden things had been inventoried and packed away for family or for sale; everything extra had been boxed and labeled. Special things that I might want had been stored separately, awaiting my final word. The love here was all in providence (provide-ance) even to extra boxes, labels, and string in case I should need them. The house, modestly furnished when my parents and I lived there, had become spartan in Aunt Louise's term. She would have said sufficient. Sufficient, but no more; even joy and grief, love and despair. What was useful was saved, the rest had no place.

Chris had noticed a drive-in movie between Solon and the place we used to go to in Oak Gap. It was for the summer only and wouldn't open for another week. He had already begun to "feel Solon" as the kids used to say—a trapped, restless feeling.

"What's to do around here? There's no TV in this dumb house and the radio's just junk and weather reports."

I was about to suggest a walk when I heard something tapping on the screen door at the front of the house. I got up and walked from the kitchen, going close, but not able to see who it was standing in the dark outside. The voice, when it came, was my youth, my growing up, and at last, my leaving.

"Luz, you there?"

"Alice? Alice, is that you?"

I threw the door open for her and she came into the light. For a minute I thought it was a joke, a trick of the mind or the light or the neighbors.

My friend, Alice Barrientos, had been lean, high-strung, and wild. She was everything that Solon wasn't: quick to anger and forgiveness, laughing and crying too freely for Solon's measuring ways, too generous and forgetful for its provide-ance. This woman was squat, contained; an ordinary, placid, middle-aged wife and mother. I saw tolerance and warmth in her face, a solid face; but in Alice's voice, the woman said, "It's me—Honest, Luz, *really.*"

She laughed, but there was an edge of hurt, and because I knew why she was hurt, and that it had nothing to do with vanity but with fidelity, I knew her for my friend Alice, whatever face and body she had grown into. I laughed and hugged her to me, catching the odor of work and warm kitchens. As striking as she had been, Alice was never proud or careful of her looks. She was only afraid that I might be ashamed of her, now that I had grown away from Solon and into the world of wealth and choice. Ken and Chris came in then, and I introduced my best friend Alice, watching their confusion mask itself at their differing rates of speed.

In the days before it mattered, before it meant death and shame, the Muriu brothers used to chase us along the beaches from Spanish Beds to the Landing, and I had told Ken and Chris the story, making it innocent for them. By common agreement, the Portuguese used the clam beds that lay west of Solon Landing, three or four miles down the rocky coast. Spanish Beds were "their" clamming, Spanish Cove, "their" place. Anyone younger or weaker learned to fear the Murius, but my friendship with Alice brought me under their eyes and made both of us a special cause with them. If we went clamming together anywhere near them and a Muriu saw us, it meant a desperate race or a half-drowning in the sea. I knew that here in this living room, my husband and son were trying to see us racing, to squint us into those girls about whom I had told the stories. Was this my gay, impulsive friend Alice, her feet toughened even to the broken glass that Summer People left from picnics along the inlet? I was sure that neither of us could run a quarter of a mile today without gasping.

We made her sit down for coffee and then Ken tried to excuse himself so that we would be free to talk.

"Oh, no, listen," Alice said, and waved a competent housewife's hand. "I can't stay. I got Charlie home watchin' the kids, and I said I wouldn't stay but only to say hello. It's Charlie Conyers, you know, that's my husband." She said it quietly, with a touch of wonder.

"But when can I see you?" I asked.

Her smile remembered her.

"I tell you what—Charlie's ma goes to Batavia every Thursday to see the doctor. If you come over in the afternoon, I'll get the kids out of the way somehow and we can have tea and talk—just talk about things. . . ." Her voice was hushed.

I had forgotten that fact of life—the isolation of Solon's farm women. Their days were busy with work and children, but even in summer with tourists crowding the roads and clogging the stores and the wharf, they came and went quickly, set apart from the romances the Summer People made of their lives. Waiting in stores, the farm women seemed to look through eyes widened with wordlessness and solitude. How could I have forgotten them, sitting in the old Fords, all with the same dished-in posture, nursing a baby or hushing a fretful child? They had been the specters of my youth, and now my friend Alice—a woman who would starve and go bare before she begged a cent of charity—invited me to tea in a voice that pleaded.

"Luz," Chris said afterward. "She called you Luz."

"My nickname," I said. "Nicknames invoke things that seem silly later. Off Spanish Beds there's a shoal called Kemble's Shoal on maps, but the Portuguese who sail there call it Cerco San Luz—The Barrier of St. Luz. In first grade, Alice heard me called Luce, and asked the teacher if I was the Barrier Luz."

Chris looked at me almost clinically, his eyes interested. I wanted to tell him that his having climbed Selden's Peak to stay all night would not be believed by his children; that his having once been a small boy would not be believed either. Instead, I gathered up the coffee cups for washing.

It was a successful farm, Conyers'. When I drove up in front of it, I tried to resist the old Solon habit of evaluating everything, but my eye picked it all out and my mind leaped willfully to judge and measure: good fences, new machinery, the old ugly outbuildings gone, flowers around the house. In my time, flowers around a farmhouse were the surest mark of prosperity. They meant that the farmer could afford to grow things he didn't have to eat or sell, and that his wife had the leisure to cultivate what had no purpose but beauty.

I was barely out of the car when Alice came bouncing around the side of the house waving to me, smiling. She looked smaller and neater in the daylight, and she was leading a little child by the hand. I remembered Mr. Peregoy's description and wanted to laugh. As far as anyone could remember, there had always been a Conyers look; the boys grew into it, the girls passed it on. The Conyers were sandy-haired and wide-headed with ruddy, apple-cheeked complexions and clear blue eyes. This Conyers would never be lost in a family portrait; he was black and gold with a smile that shut both eyes.

I called across the space between us, "Alice, he's beautiful!" She put her head back and laughed, and I realized that she had read my thoughts and agreed without shame; the child looked nothing at all like Charlie or like Charlie's kin.

We sat over tea, talking about this and that, and I felt an extra weight in the things we said, like the words war veterans use years later.

"Alice, you've done wonders here—the flowers, the house——"

"Well"—she shrugged—"Charlie's ma didn't want it changed none in the beginning, but when the babies started to come, I just got to having notional fits. First I had to have bright curtains and then I got to needing flowers around me." Her eyes were shrewd. "You *know* how pregnant women are—how they have to get what they need. Later, when Dale was on the way, I started to have these real bad dreams about the old shacks out front, and I got scared it would mark the baby, me havin' bad dreams. . . ." We laughed. "I reckon they're used to seein' all the way to the road now. And too, things are better for us. Charlie does winter work in town and we been sellin' things to the Summer People —fruit and vegetables and the extra when I make pickles or jelly. Charlie's changed some of his dad's ways. We quit havin' hay on the place here and bought Wingate's field."

I looked up quickly, but her face showed no change. It could have been anyone's field, anywhere.

"Wingate's field?" I asked.

"Yes, he finally let it go. Summers whenever I can, I like to take the kids over and let them play in that stream down there. You probably forgot, but I remember all the good times we had, you and me, pickin' berries." Her face was soft with contentment.

"I remember Wingate's field," I said. "I wish I could forget it. I used to dream about it, and sometimes I still do—how that dead girl lay there in the stream and we couldn't go and pull her out; and how scared we were that somebody in the gang would look around and see us or hear us breathing and come for us. And sometimes I wonder if she died because we couldn't get help for her, or take her out of there. Alice, I know it's nonsense, but I don't think I could ever take a child of mine to play in Wingate's field."

She was looking at me keenly, her face full of sympathy. "Lucy, you never told me such a bad thing happened there. When was it? Did anyone hurt you?"

"Alice, you can't be serious. . . . Not me—us—you and I, hiding from the Muriu Brothers and John Fatika, and that Anna, that girl of John's——"

"I don't remember anything like that," she said, shaking her head. "When was it?"

"We were twelve. I'd just started having my periods and I was so self-conscious I thought everyone could tell just by looking at me. I was having one then, and I remember being terrified that somehow with all the blood from that girl, that they would sense my blood and come and find us and kill us. . . ."

She was nodding very slowly. "Did you ever tell me? . . . I remember you tellin' me one time . . . somethin'. . . ."

"You were there with me, Alice, hiding right by the tree. We were bent down together, hidden by the overhanging branch and by the vines that grew up thick there, close to the water."

Her eyes were puzzled and faraway. "Wasn't there a Summer Girl, a girl—some girl wearin' white shorts and a little——" Her hand made the pantomime of a halter—a kerchief, really—folded on the bias so the two short ends would separate and tie around the neck and the long side go around the midriff.

Something made me resent Alice's smugness, her forgetting, the easy glossing over of what had cost me a dozen nightmares and another dozen daytime confrontations with guilt and sorrow. Or could it be that my memory was a dream or a lie, something that would give me a reason for fleeing a place so idyllic that people flocked to it in summer for peace and renewing? Alice was the only one who could know if it was real and not a story; we had shut all the other doors to truth ourselves.

"What color was that halter?" I said, and the words came out severely, like those of a teacher impatient with a balky student.

"Dots," Alice said vaguely. "Red and white."

I nodded slowly.

"Listen, Luz—I do remember something. . . . Were there some people, the Muriu brothers, and like you said, John Fatika and a girl? And they come there when we was pickin' berries. To have a picnic . . ." Her face was clouded and she sat up tensely at the clean kitchen table in the bright, clean, happy house. Her voice, when it came again, was full of shock and sorrow. "Mother of God, I forgot that bad thing!"

It was too late to stop, but I wished then that I could. Had I come back to Solon after eighteen years to give my friend unnecessary pain and then tell myself it was for the sake of truth? Alice was remembering it now, her eyes distant and brooding, the lines deepening at the brows. "Somethin' was wrong, wasn't it, Luz, or else why did we hide when they come?"

"It was that girl, John's girl, Anna. She was ahead of us, in eighth grade, but she'd been left back so many times she might have been sixteen—and four boys with her, boys eighteen, who were used to having what they wanted. . . . Wasn't it funny they would go without Marta or Veronica or even their sisters . . . to a picnic?"

"Luz!" Like a little cry. Then it was true.

I said, "Yes, Alice," and was strangely relieved.

"That girl walked by, in her shorts and that top, and they waved to her and said, 'Come on sit here a minute', and they was all smilin' and laughin', so she went——"

"Alice, I never asked you, but it was always on my mind to ask you what you heard Anna say just then."

"I remember it . . . it was somethin' dirty. The boys was laughin'. We got scared, so we stayed. At first they didn't do nothin' bad, just laughed, but she started to get scared. Then——"

"Wait, don't say any more——"

"But Jesus-Mary, Luz, you got me rememberin', and it's like it's happening now, because I can't stop what I'm seeing in my mind—the boys tearin' her top off and how she was runnin' right near where we was, and cryin' and the boys . . . they stopped a minute, like they got sorry they hurt her and they was ashamed. Why didn't they stop then? Why didn't they let her go?"

I couldn't stop either, or let Alice go, because it was that summer day that had changed Solon for me, and had changed me. "Don't you remember what happened then?"

"Anna?" she ventured. "Something with Anna . . ."

"It was what she said." I wanted to tell Alice simply, not to make high drama out of it, since that kind of drama is only the taking of the stage away from those to whom it really belongs, but after all the years of dreaming and thinking, I needed to see how much had been changed by me beyond my knowing. It was hard to take away all the feeling that had been built up and leave only the words. "She said to them, 'Are you men, or what?' "

Alice looked up at me, her eyes full of tears. "I remember now. She was actin' like somebody in a book or somethin', like they would be cowards if that girl got away."

"Oh, Alice, I'm sorry, so sorry."

She put her head down on the table and began to sob. I knew I couldn't ask her about the rest, about our part in the things that happened afterwards.

I heard a little scratching at the kitchen door and I went and got a glass of water for the thirsty child who was waiting there. Alice had stopped crying, but I kept my body between her and the child's eyes. When Chris was this child's age, he needed the sight of me, the touch of me in a kind of tidal rhythm, in and out again. I remembered it clearly. I had to deny this child. He stuck out his lip and moved back a step, guardedly. I closed the door.

"Alice, I never meant to come back and rake all this up. I guess I couldn't understand how you could forget it all—how anyone could forget a thing like that. Maybe I thought—I don't know what, but I hope you'll forgive me for doing this."

She had wiped her eyes and composed her face, but now it was puzzled. "Luz, you know, sometimes I didn't understand the things you used to say and do. I used to think it was because you was raised down the beach and not like our people. You been wonderin' why I forgot that awful thing. I been sittin' here wonderin' why you remembered it."

"It's not a choice," I said. "It's how I am. Sometimes I dream about what happened, and now and then I remember parts of it. If it seems to come back more these days than it did when I was growing up or starting out on my own, it's because I've been very happy——"

The puzzled look deepened. "Why would anybody want to keep all that junk in her mind? Now you say it's because you're *happy?*" Her stubby, competent hands came up in a gesture I remembered from times before I knew how to read or write.

"Alice, it's not something I *decided* to do. I could no more stop remembering than you could stop forgetting, but it *is* happiness that brings it back. When I was first married, there were money worries and then all the busy time of housekeeping and having a baby. It's in the quiet room, the quiet mind, that you remember, and then sometimes questions come." I

couldn't tell her the questions I had about that day—
they seemed suddenly too complicated. "They're questions of conscience, that's all."

Alice was suddenly maternal. "Listen, Luz, you think
it was so easy for me? Charlie's ma was never too
crazy about me and one of the reasons was, she
was scared everybody in Spanish Cove would move in
here. I had to tell her I didn' care about nobody back
there and I wouldn't see none of my sisters or cousins
after I moved here. What was I supposed to do? Forget
them? Now, what I do, I wait for old man Bontecou
to come by on his way to town. I go out and get something from him, one thing at a time, and he tells me
messages and I send messages with him. Then, Saturdays, I go shopping quick and I go to Oak Gap instead
of Solon so I can stop by home and see how everyone
is."

Alice must have thought I was criticizing her life. If
not, why did she feel she had to defend it? I knew
then that the questions could never be shared, that
nothing could be weighed with the other witness. She
would forgive me for the pain I had caused her; all I
had to do was accept.

"Alice, you don't mean to tell me that Old Man
Bontecou is still driving that truck of his!"

Her face eased, her smiled warmed, "Luz, you
wouldn't believe it . . ." She leaned forward. "Remember his brother, that Ferdy. . . ."

"We were getting worried," Ken said. "We nearly
called the cops."

It would be Sheriff Blankenship, if he was still
here, not the strangers who had come, after the murder,
to question us because Mr. Wingate had seen us in his
field that morning, picking berries. The police had been
hard, tired strangers, and in fear of the Murius and of
Anna, I had lied to them, and when they threatened
me, I had felt justified and lied more. I found out later

that Alice had lied too, but why, or at what cost, I never knew because we didn't speak of that day again. Now I was finding it hard to shake myself free of it.

"What?" I said.

"It's so late—you've been gone for hours."

"We got talking," I said, "and then I drove for a while."

I was thinking and suddenly I knew what I wanted. I almost smiled, thinking of Alice's "messages" with Old Man Bontecou. "We don't have a thing in the house, so I'm going to hop down to Peregoy's before it closes." And before anyone had a chance to say anything, I was gone.

The store still had a little drift of late shoppers. Again I stood before Mr. Peregoy and called his name. Again he looked up grimly, again broke into the smile, the greeting. I saw that he was enjoying it as much as I—the belonging, making the distinction plain between his loyalties.

I asked about some of my old schoolmates, circling in slowly so as not to alarm him or make him wonder later why I should have wanted to know. "It's hard to think of Julia having five kids. I remember her going with Fred in school, and of course him on the team. Fred's class made quite a team—Alec Soames and Nick Bedlow, and one of the Muriu brothers. . . . What ever happened to those tough Muriu boys?"

He thought a moment, during which I tried to make my face bland and my heart slow. Then he said, almost in wonder, "Why, I don't know. . . . I don't think they're down at the Cove any more. That Alice—like I told you—she went and married Charlie Conyers."

"I know," I said. "I stopped by today and saw her. She's done wonders with the place."

I couldn't help saying that. It was his having lumped Alice with the Murius that made me say it. I waited a while longer, asking about others, and then I took the few things I'd bought and went out into what was now full dark.

We left Solon the next day. Riding toward Oak Gap where the real-estate man waited for Aunt Louise's keys, we saw the Summer People. Their bright colors seemed to fill the landscape, to overwhelm it. Large women in small bikinis sunned beside pools; loud-shirted men and boys in clothes too new and colors too bright fished restlessly from the bridges; campers and hikers came and went in the woods. Cars piled high with the demanding equipment of leisure, moved at a forced slowness down the narrow roads. Sometimes I would wait for the landmarks and cry out, usually too late, "Horners are gone! I didn't notice that coming in! . . . Look what they've done to Stite's field. . . . I wonder if that store is open all year—probably not, just for the Summer People."

"Ma, why do you hate Summer People?"

"What makes you say that? I don't hate anybody. I certainly don't hate anyone I never even met."

Chris's voice was troubled and earnest and breaking with change. "Well, maybe not *hate,* but like they're not there, like you're looking over their heads, or through them . . . like they're not even people."

I sighed, trying to think of an answer, but he went on, "It's not only you; it's all the regular people—I mean the ones who stay. It's only when they find out I'm your son that I seem to be anybody at all."

"Honey, it's so hard to tell you. You would have had to grow up here to know what it is and what it means."

"What does it mean?"

"Summer People are the ones who go home before the responsibilities set in. Their loyalties are some-where else. They want to be free of care, but care is also caring. Summer People don't know the names of the trees. No one they love or hate is buried here. . . ."

"Well, just remember," he said righteously, "that back in Solon, *I'm* Summer People."

"But not everywhere," I said quickly, "Not everywhere. Somewhere you stay and fight the battles; you pay the price somewhere; somewhere you bear the weight."

Chris looked at me, puzzled.

Ken said, "We bring 'em up as though we want them to be Summer People, don't we? And then we're horrified when they are."

"What are you talking about?" Chris said, frightened, as he now was, about obligation and compromise.

"Listen, son," Ken said. "We're saying that there really are things waiting for you to learn." Then he turned to me, smiling, "And you, Barrier Luz, can't you be Summer People somewhere?"

5   The Supremacy of the Hunza

MARGOLIN'S HOUSE WAS four miles down Ridge Road, and part of his keen pleasure in coming home each day was in turning off the highway onto its blacktop. It was a slow road, one of the old wagon trails, lined with trees and made without the raw wounds of blasting. The way wound through hills, past meadows and upland pastures. Turning north, a wide vista opened on blue-dark pine mountains, and then the way turned down and Margolin took the dirt road to the right, to home.

It was an old house, square but leaning in its age as the ground did. Marbles put down by Margolin's youngest boy rolled west in some rooms, east in others, as though the center of the earth was in some question. The rear of the house looked out over the pine hills and back the way Margolin had come. He and Regina and never owned land or a house before this one. Because of its age, its place, and its view, Regina lived with the house's ancient crochets and Margolin became a commuter, submitting to the shocking erosion of his leisure time in travel. It was worth it, they told their incredulous friends. There might not be much time, but there was a sense of time here, and of stillness. Then the power-towers came.

The first was neatly placed, whole, while Margolin was at work. It stood ninety feet tall and gleaming silver at the side of Ridge Road. The next day there were two; then five. Then there was a row of towers across the road and down in hundred-foot strides. They climbed hills, walked valleys; they were hung with great muscles of cable. Two-hundred foot swaths were cut through the woods to accommodate them until they stood in a cable-hung line fifteen miles long, crossing all the forest and hill country between Emmettstown and Hale.

Margolin felt invaded, betrayed. He called the Power Company and was told that the land was a long-purchased right-of-way. He called his lawyer, who looked into it and found that the land had been deeded in 1913, when there had been no zoning statutes, and that the owners were held only by what applied at the time of purchase. Margolin hung up, fuming.

"There's nothing we can do," Regina said. "We'll just have to learn not to see them, that's all."

"That's the whole point!" he raged. "We came here so we wouldn't have to un-see everything. They have no right to make us un-see the damn things! They could have buried the cables and they know it!" When a neighbor called and told him about the protest meeting, Margolin was eager to go.

Regina shrugged, "The law is on their side—I think it's useless to fight it."

"But if we *all* protest——"

"Okay," she said. "Okay."

So he sat on the familiar folding chair in the school gym and waited for the meeting to start. Regina was right. What could they hope to do? The Company was within its rights; its eyesore towers were on its own land, owned long before the people who wanted to see these hills and meadows had come and begun to destroy them with houses. A man can spend his lifetime protesting and petitioning but there can never be any real protection for the ephemeral, unnamable joys of life. Across the gym a man stood up and waved to him. He saw it was Larry Westercamp.

Margolin seldom saw Westercamp except at meetings. There had been the school battles over sex education and busing and bomb shelters before this. The Margolins had gone dutifully to be counted, but Westercamp and his wife seemed to come alive in the atmosphere of organized complaint. They had been on numberless peace marches and zoning protests; their anger instantly took form as a petition, and in the meetings Westercamp was always at the core of the group, passionate and indignant and demanding action. Now he was coming over. Margolin sighed and began automatically to formulate an excuse. The meeting wouldn't end before midnight, and now he had Westercamp too.

Watching the lithe man move across the gym, Margolin realized that part of his irritation was envy. Westercamp was over forty and there wasn't an ounce of flab on him. His face had a striking, ascetic angularity; it was a face popularly imagined on poets and saints. Margolin was slightly sagging in the middle; he wore glasses and was getting bald, but Westercamp's hair was a magnificent steely-gray mass which he tossed in moments of restlessness, like a proud horse or a boy.

"Hi!" and he came over, smiling. He always seemed delighted to see Margolin and sat down beside him with a neatness that made Margolin feel older. "Ave's home with the kids," he whispered. "Measles."

"Oh?" Margolin said.

"She wanted to come, but measles can be serious, you know."

"Yes, I know." Margolin nodded.

"The doctors around here are prejudiced by their union. They're against anyone who wants to keep his health by natural means. Drugs, vaccination—it's all they know. We've had the kids on vitamin C to build them up. The school nurse called us fanatics."

"Oh, well," Margolin said, grateful for something on which he had no opinion.

The meeting began. The problem of the towers was described in agonizing detail. Their height and distance, number of lines and voltage was argued for over an hour. Everyone who said "ninety-foot towers" was reminded by someone else that the towers were ninety-three feet eight inches. Westercamp was often on his feet, explaining, urging. A woman said the towers might be a safety hazard and then the question of their falling or the lines falling was argued for another hour.

At the beginning Margolin sat listening in excruciating impatience. Slowly, his restlessness thickened into a kind of leaden boredom which turned down gentling as it released itself toward sleep. His head moved forward, his arms relaxed. Behind him a chair scraped and he shot up, shocked into wakefulness, not sure where he was. Beside him Westercamp was following each anguished point and question with alertness, rising to explain and embroil himself in each side issue.

At last the meeting broke up, having settled nothing but that there would have to be another meeting to decide the main thrust of the protest. It was very late and people left quickly. Margolin was tired and disgusted. He hung back out of boredom, staring at the display of children's art work on the walls above the gym equipment.

When his eye had worked itself twice around the

empty room, he knew it was time to go, and he forced himself out through the back door of the gym and into the darkness. The night air brought him awake. He breathed in deeply and found himself smiling. He stretched and felt the air widening in his lungs. Suddenly he was alert and hungry, his senses keen. The autumn wind had sharpened the edges of everything; a wind-apple scent twisted past him from the orchard farms on the other side of town. There was late-cut grass too, and as he turned, a faint, resinous smell— pine trees from the woods miles west of where he stood. He was smiling, relishing the night and his solitude and how ancient a pleasure it was to sort the scents of the wind. He was sorry he had brought the car. It would have been good to walk the three miles home, warming himself from the work of it. He looked out toward the parking lot. Beyond it stood the line of towers, now with red lights on top of them to warn away aircraft. The pyramid, he thought and sighed, the most stable structure there is. They were in for good and a million meetings wouldn't move them.

"Civilization!" He jumped. The voice was Westercamp's, behind him. Damn! Margolin felt caught at something. He turned and there was Westercamp pointing to the towers. "Why do we let ourselves be used by these . . . gadgets. . . . America's gone soft."

"I don't like the towers either," Margolin said uneasily. He didn't want to hear about Soft America. Searching for something else, he remembered a half-heard fragment of table conversation. "Hey, the kids say they saw you on TV. How does it feel to be in Show Biz?" He saw he had said the wrong thing.

Westercamp tossed his head nervously and dug his hands into his pockets. "It's just another part of what I've been trying to fight; the mechanization, the reduction of everything. The news media made a big joke of it."

THE SUPREMACY OF THE HUNZA 131

Margolin wished he had remembered more of what his children had said. "Uh—I didn't see it. What happened?"

"Our section in Fish and Game has been working on a new strain of brook trout. We needed a species with a high tolerance for the common pollutants. Last week the Governor invited the four other governors here for those Regional Conservation talks of his. We were supposed to give a demonstration of the trout, but we didn't know it was rigged as a stunt. They announced that the Five Governors were going to do a little fishing, that away from all the pressures and publicity they might be able to work out the issues. Then Fish and Game got the word that the Governors had better catch something, and what better than the new trout? I had to take almost all of our new fish upstream of their 'secluded spot' and release them to be dragged out three hundred feet away."

"That's kind of standard, isn't it?" Margolin said. "Honor of the State and all that?"

"There were newsmen in that 'secluded spot' taking pictures of me throwing the fish *in* and others taking pictures of the Governors pulling them *out*. On the six-o'clock news they mentioned the specially developed trout, and they mentioned conservation talks, but nobody paid attention. It was a big comedy. They had spliced my section and the Governor's sections together and speeded up the film. They even set it to music. Me throwing and them catching. It looked like a sort of dance, fixed in rhythm, in, out, my face, the Governor's faces, and then the fish, so we were all doing a kind of dance."

Margolin had begun to laugh. He couldn't help it. He imagined the look on the faces of the men and on the faces of the fish. The Governors were clad in skins, grunting as they pulled out fish in a steadily quickening rhythm, Westercamp working faster and faster, the wide-eyed fish more and more confused. He tried to stop and tell Westercamp that he wasn't laughing at him or his job. The man just stood there looking wounded until Margolin forced himself to stop and offer a ride home. The answer was stiff, but Margolin hadn't wanted to be cruel and Westercamp knew it.

"I'm sorry, really," Margolin said. "I suppose feeling strongly about a thing puts it out of the joking category." They got into the car.

Westercamp, still earnest, persisted, "It's just that you, of all people, must know how important it is—not only conservation, but human—dignity. The average man doesn't see, but you're an anthropologist; you study uncorrupted people, people who live as nature intended. . . ."

For a minute Margolin didn't understand. "What?"

"I mean you can see how far we've gone from the true pattern, the way people were meant to live."

Margolin turned out on the road and then glanced at Westercamp. "Larry, all men impose a pattern on nature. The lives of the people I study are often more artificially determined than ours. I just study the pattern, I'm not looking for Utopia."

"But there are people whose lives aren't complicated by—by . . ." and he gestured out the window to the few lights in a deserted shopping center.

"I don't know that it's better to have a life complicated by dead ancestors whose clan taboos must be remembered and followed——"

"I'm not saying that others don't go wrong—tribes full of superstition and fear, but there are others, certain groups . . ."

They pulled up at Westercamp's house. Margolin wondered if he should shut off the motor. It was late and he was tired, but he didn't want to seem impatient or draw attention to his waiting. Westercamp was still working. "Doesn't it disturb you that we—the richest nation on earth—are plagued with mental illness, moral decay, pollution of our air, our water, our values—?" He was aware that he had lost a connecting point in his idea. "Well, you *understand*," as though Margolin had only been teasing him. He looked up at the dark house, "Ave's probably gone to bed."

He opened the car door, got out, and then turned back to Margolin, "Look, we've got to fight those towers. We can't give up. Come to the meetings—we need you. People get excited at first, but after a while they drop away and without organization, we're lost. You have to be vigilant—so vigilant, all the time."

In the dashboard light, Margolin saw his tight little smile, a condemned Saint, encouraging at the fire. Then Westercamp turned and went to his house.

Margolin could see by his walk that Westercamp was tired. The youthfulness seemed to have fallen from him like a disguise, with only the physical props still there, the hunting boots, the soft old shirt with half-rolled sleeves; young Estercamp forever just returning from the woods strong and uncompromised. Except that suddenly the forty-three-year-old man was in disguise and admitting to his age. Margolin wondered why he should be so comforted by that admission.

He headed home, keeping the window down and trying to relive some of the enjoyment he had had in the beauty of the night. Now it was only cold and late and going to be hard to get up tomorrow. "Primitive man!" he muttered. Then he thought about Westercamp again, beautifully choreographed, feeding fish to the Governors' mountain stream, and by the time he got home, he had orchestrated in order, a minuet, a tango, a wild "primitive" native dance.

In following weeks the Margolins began to get phone calls and mail from some of Westercamp's conservation groups. Regina laughed at Margolin's "new hobby," but he found himself inordinately angry at Westercamp's violation of his privacy. The letters and calls were so importunate, so desperate and convinced: Did he know that Strontium 90 was building up in our bodies? Did he know that the water table was dropping, the world was burning its resources, wastes were poisoning its soil, war eroding its morals? *Act Now!* He put the pamphlets in the bottom of the filing cabinet when Regina wasn't looking.

The second meeting about the towers was held on an evening when Margolin had to be at the University and he was relieved not to have to go. The next day Westercamp called. "Ted, I didn't see you last night. I hope you haven't been sick or something."

"No, I had to stay over at school."

"I hope you can make it next time. We're getting up a petition. Frank Armbruster is going to see if we have good grounds for a lawsuit and he'll let us know."

"Uh—Larry, I've been caulking the windows, and I left things where the kids——"

But Westercamp wasn't listening. "It's going to pick up this time. This time we'll make them see. Oh, and I was talking to someone there and we got into a discussion about the Chontals. That's the way you pronounce it, isn't it, Chontals?"

"Who?"

"Chontals, those Indians on the southern Isthmus of Mexico——"

"Oh?" Margolin tried to sound professional and interested, but he was fighting an annoyance out of all proportion to the cause. Spontaneous Discussion of the Chontal. He sighed.

"I was reading," Westercamp went on, "about this man who went there. He never saw an adult strike a child. Crime and insanity don't exist there. He never saw violence. The people live on their land simply and in peace. He saw women of seventy and eighty carrying water in huge jugs for miles without tiring. I admire people who can live like that—simply. Don't you think that's wonderful?"

Margolin wanted to say, "Yes, wonderful," and go upstairs and caulk windows and curse, but he couldn't conquer his irritation. "I've never visited that group," he said, "but I know the area. I'll lay you odds that the 'women of seventy' were thirty and *looked* seventy. Employment means staying alive till tomorrow; the absence of crime is the absence of an idea of private ownership. The harmony is chronic malnutrition, the tranquility is cocoa-leaf."

"Ulcers and heart trouble are unknown," Westercamp argued doggedly. "Diabetes and mental illness——"

But Margolin couldn't stop either. "They have rickets, pellagra, TB, smallpox. The infant-mortality rate culls out everyone but natural survivors. Mental illness 'exists' only where people accept the possibility of changing human behavior."

"But diseases like rickets are cured by decent diet, medical knowledge that we——"

"Larry, if the Good Life depends on decent diet and medicine, then the Good Life isn't Chontal, is it?"

"Well what about Tristan, then, Tristan de Cunha?" The big proof, the cap.

"What about it?" Margolin said, remembering the magazine stories. "The Islanders were warned and later evacuated to Liverpool because an earthquake had been predicted."

"Yes," shouted Westercamp in triumph, "but they found themselves getting cavities in their teeth; they saw their old people getting respiratory diseases, and their children picking up the values of the gutter; so they packed up and they got out, all of them, back to a decent life, a life away from 'civilization'!"

"After seeing six months in a Liverpool slum as 'civilization,'" Margolin said acidly. The magazines had played it Westercamp's way, he remembered: The Good Life vs. Sin & the City. "The men with the rotten teeth and bad morals were the ones whose machines had predicted the trouble and saved the Islanders in the first place. Too bad about cavities, but the people of Tristan were unskilled and illiterate in a world that demands both skill and literacy. The population in paradise is dwindling anyway, aging and dwindling, because in spite of clean air, good morals, and no cavities, the general health is poor. With a single occupation possible and almost no choice of mates, there is very little dimension to life on Tristan, because Tristan as Utopia just doesn't work. . . . OK?"

The phone-voice sounded wounded. "Well, you know more about them than I do, I guess," and Westercamp said good-bye, leaving the victory of the dead line to Margolin.

"Be as little Chontal," Margolin muttered, and hung up. His mind passed over other words to where his envy was: What right did Westercamp have to make heroes? That ugliness scared him so badly that he had to promise himself to be decent next time, and generous, and leave Westercamp's illusions alone.

In time the mailbox glut slowed a little, and it became peacefully automatic to put the tracts away in the filing cabinet. They had a place. Outside the power-towers showed no sign of departing the landscape, and Margolin tried his best to ignore them, look through them, adjust them to his eye in some automatic way, but none of the tricks worked. He missed the third meeting and the fourth, and after that he wasn't called again.

The autumn moved from abundance to its lean old age. The trees shriveled and darkened, the frosts fell dry. Winds screamed in the towers. Margolin began to have daydreams about those towers blowing over; they were juvenile, self-indulgent dreams and they made him ashamed. Then it snowed and the towers stood out like skeleton sentries overwhelming the hills where they stalked, watching. They had been up for five months. He knew they would never come down; he knew that defacing the land with them was wrong, in Westercamp's word, unnatural, and that there was nothing he could do.

It worried Regina to see him sitting in the chair by the window, looking out dully as an invalid at trees, sky, and the graffiti of birds and small animals in the snow. The sun picked out the towers in a blue-white blaze. He knew she was able to strike their ugliness from her mind. If she had been asked to draw the meadow in front of their house and the hills stretching beyond, her painstaking sketch would have shown no towers. They had spoken about her gift for ignoring ugliness once or twice, and when he thought about it, it frightened him. Now it was one of her sources of strength. He thought she might try to coax him away from the betrayal by keeping him busy. His special project was coming in December. He would be home until then.

He was correct. She began to invite people over for dinner, for cards, for nothing. Soon the guests reciprocated until every evening was filled, until he complained that he didn't have enough time for his reading or his work. What was the matter with her? Why was she so restless?

It was at one of these automatically reciprocating forced marches that he saw Westercamp again. Remembering his stubborness he thought that Westercamp might turn away, but whatever losses Westercamp had suffered, he seemed to have forgotten them and he hurried over smiling to greet Margolin, "Ted, hi!"

"Hi, Larry," he said. "How's it going?"

"Fine, fine," and Westercamp grinned. They went over to get drinks and Margolin dug around for something to talk about. "Say, how is the group coming on the towers?" Westercamp gave the dip of his head that showed he was embarrassed.

"Well, it's just about disbanded. . . ." Margolin realized the embarrassment was for him—one of the Righteous who hadn't been there.

"We had too few coming to make a real fight of it," Westercamp added. "We did make some calls; we sent the petition and Armbruster is still looking into the legal angle, but"—and his taut, ascetic's face gave a quick twitch of a smile—"people aren't willing to back up their beliefs."

"Oh, come on, Larry!" Margolin said. "A well-led group could have gotten it done in fifteen minutes, and instead of group therapy we could have had our petition going right away. I went to the meeting to register a protest, not start a career. There was no firm leadership and we got bogged down in side issues. The thing didn't die of apathy, but of incompetence."

Westercamp stared at him with the shock of having heard something obscene. Margolin muttered an excuse and slipped away.

The Margolins left early. It was a thick, ugly night. As they came toward home, he looked around for the towers, but they were hidden in fog; even the mean-eyed red lights. "Damn things! I hurt Larry again, Reg, but he's so naive!"

"Then why are you so hard on him? Why can't you leave him alone?"

"I don't know. He's using me, and . . . I don't know."

He escaped into work gratefully. It was almost time for Christmas vacation and he had been asked by a therapist at the State Hospital to spend some time with three Sioux who were patients there. "They dream," the therapist had said, "and I'm out of my depth with the symbols they're using."

Margolin had been looking forward to going. It would be a relief to be called from the twilight window where he could see the towers closing upon his house. Perhaps he might be able to help in some way, although he was no expert on the Sioux. Some insight here might freshen his classes, anyway.

When the day came, he packed delightedly and told Regina that he would come back rested and stimulated and looking forward to writing *Acculturation* on the blackboard again. He left earlier than he needed with a feeling of excitement, as though he were going to set off cross-country to a place unmapped but where all Towers were his to deal with. He called her from a hotel near the Hospital and a few times after that to find out if everything was all right, and he called her when he was getting ready to leave. His voice on the phone hadn't prepared her for the way he looked when he walked into the house again, He stood without moving, gray and sick and deeply tired, so changed that she was stunned and couldn't think of anything to say. For a while they simply stared at each other. "Ted?"

"Hi."

"Darling, what happened? You look exhausted."

"Tomorrow," he said, "not now."

"Let me take your coat—come on in the kitchen and have some coffee. It's all ready. . . ."

The whole house had been readied for his home-coming; Regina in her diaphanous blue thing, the kids in bed, the rooms orderly. He sat in the quiet room with his coffee and realized that as exhausted as he was, he wouldn't sleep. He was afraid even to try.

After a while she asked, "Did you have a nice room at the hotel?"

"It was fine." Then he laughed, shaking his head at the lie he was beginning; he would have to tell her something, and if it wasn't what had happened, it would have to be some kind of lie. "It wasn't fine," he said. "I can't even remember what it was like. What I remember is a series of gray-smelling interview rooms, two senile old Sioux and Benton Song." He spoke slowly, seeing himself again in those rooms, listening as he had, cold and alone, to tapes of Benton breaking asunder with astonishing dreams. In the nightmare landscape's vastness, the symbols of The People had become cheapened parodies, like the Made in Japan trinkets Benton sold summers from a plastic wigwam off the highway.

"Start at the beginning," she said.

"In the first place, Benton isn't Sioux at all. He comes from Arizona; his mother was Navaho, his father one of the Tewa living in Taos Pueblo. At the staff-meeting they talked about The Indians, not Navaho or Tewa. Benton is the product of a marriage like that of a Japanese geisha and a Sicilian grape-grower. I tried to help him, Reg, and I couldn't. I didn't patronize him or play the scholar, but I couldn't help either. In the middle of our first meeting he got up and yelled, 'Your mother is full of cowboy pictures!' and left."

"What happened? Did he come back again?"

"No, I went to see him on the ward. We talked there at first. He needed all kinds of proofs of my honesty and competence—you can't give that in two weeks and he knew I had that time limit, that neat vacation, 'two weeks with The Savages,' he said. There've been too many fake-authentic Indian things and too many bad books. Even the simple facts of Benton's life give him pain. Sometimes he was—well, never mind. His mother was a professional Indian, going around the country to march in parades and 'do' conventions while his father waited back in Taos and wondered why his wife couldn't be the way women are supposed to be. Later she took Benton on tour with her."

"But that's no Indian background—it's . . . nothing."

"It was this Indian's background—" and he smiled sourly. "At one time I did try to pin him to a category—'With which people were you most at home?' He only shouted at me: 'With the warriors of the Silver Screen! Apaches in feathers, bathing trunks under their breechclouts, Sioux in sneakers. Tonto, him my brother!'

"I tried to make him see that even his mixed symbols had meanings that Anglos might not know: 'The hawks you see in Dr. Ferrier's tests and the ones you dream about— he's trying to find a way to help you . . .' He answered, 'I don't know about that! They threw me out before the movie ended!'"

"You can't be expected to do psychoanalysis in two weeks," Regina said, defending him.

"I was supposed to know the context of those dreams —to show Ferrier where the symbols carried cultural weight." He began to repeat one of the dreams that Benton, tonguetied with tranquilizers had given to the tape recorder to haunt Margolin's evenings:

"The sky is clear—it's someplace near Window Rock. It's noon and the sun is riding the world. Something is going to happen, but I don't know what, and I'm afraid it's a sign I won't see or recognize—that I'll miss it. I'm sitting on a mesa, a small mesa, all piled with rocks, alone. I'm watching everything, and I'm watching me. I'm born from the sun—I look down and see the me that's down there, far, far down. I'm a hawk. I despise that crawling thing so far down there. I begin to dive toward it, to kill it, and I feel a heat and a chill in me, a kind of crying, like crying for air when you can't breathe. I open my big wings and my shadow darkens the man and the rock. What the wanting is— it's to join that shadow—to be all one. I scream, dive head-on toward myself, man and shadow, and hawk, all one, and when I hit, it's dying, the end—a terrible pain, and I wake up."

"It has a beauty to it," Regina said.

He sighed. "I suppose it has." He looked around at the kitchen, shining and clean for his homecoming. "There are tribal realities in it, and universal ones, and a self-wounding satire of the White Man's Red Man, and I can't really tell where one leaves off and another begins. We soon stopped having 'interview' and just talked; that is, when we could. He would fight on the ward at night sometimes. Then he would come in the next day black and blue and groggy with drugs. I liked him, so it hurt—that business. Before I left this morning, I stopped in to say good-bye and we shook hands. I hadn't thought he would commit himself like that. I wanted something—anything that could make it better for him. He's intelligent and he knows it in spite of all the 'injun-talk.' I told him to help Ferrier and the Group Therapy people by telling them about the differences between Navaho and Tewa, not letting them get away with phony symbols and a phony reality. He shook his head, and said, 'Maybe it's better to be a character in a white man's movie. When the Eagle speaks for my life what language will he use? A language I don't know? A language nobody knows any more?

"I told him to keep trying to hear the words. He looked at me and shrugged and said that at least I had been a change from sitting around on the ward, and we laughed. Then very quietly he said, 'You tried.' I—uh—gave him our address and told him to come and see us when he got out. . . . Don't worry, he won't. He folded the paper up very carefully and put it away, but we both knew he wouldn't come."

"Oh, Ted, you don't know. Maybe he will. Maybe you did do more than he said, even more than he knows himself, and then too, you helped the doctors——"

"Sure. I took the notes I'd made and brought them to a big hospital staff-conference. Everybody listened politely and when it was all over, they thanked me and complimented me and kidded in a very gentle way about the scholarly monographs to be derived from this source anguish."

"They tried to make you see that you had helped."

"Oh, Reg! They were pitying an amateur who couldn't fight away the awful hopelessness wound up in those damn tape-spools. They'll forget Benton isn't Sioux; they'll forget I told them I hadn't helped. They'll take the notes and make them law and do more studies on *The Mental Patient,* and I'll do 1 or 2 on *Acculturation* when I need something published, and Benton's pain is so awful and so frightening and nobody knows how to help!" Then he stood up and shook his head and went to bed, leaving Regina alone in her sexy blue, staring at his half-finished cup of coffee.

The next day was Saturday and he resolved that if he didn't want to be ministered to, he'd better stop acting like an object of pity. He dressed quickly and with a great show of heartiness, fixed the loose steps on the back porch, and took the kids out for hamburgers and a monster movie. Although there was nothing real in his good spirits, he was comforted by the deception. He was standing in well for the real owner of his life.

The movie struck him as being subtly obscene. Its symbols, which he understood more clearly than Benton Song's, were homosexual and fetishistic. Worried for his children, he questioned them afterwards about what they had seen. They answered from untroubled, open faces and spent the ride home delightedly reliving the crucial scenes with themselves the monster and the world gone small and helpless.

Regina looked at the greasy-fingered, bleary-eyed spectacle they made and her face relaxed. "Honey, I forgot to tell you last night—I put all the mail in the top drawer of the desk so it wouldn't get misplaced. There were some calls. I took the messages and they're in there too."

"I'll look at it all later" he said, and still working, went upstairs to see Mark's science project.

When he did get to it, he understood why Regina had let it wait. It was mania; Westercamp again, and oh, the air, the water, the food, outer space! the benthos off the continental shelf!. . . . And the phone calls. They had heard he was interested; did he wish to become a member? Did he know there was a group to—? a Council for—?

"Regina!"

"I had to save them for you. . . . Now, you've seen them you can throw them out."

The phone rang. It was for him. Did he know about the protest against mass shooting of elk in Wyoming? He hissed his answer into the phone and hung up. Regina was standing in the middle of the room, watching him, her hands raised slightly, defensively, and the gesture infuriated him.

"This is riduculous!" he said. "I won't have that damn fool involving me in every hysterical cause he's hooked on!" He went for the phone book to get Westercamp.

"Ted. . . . Just a minute. I think you should know—something's happened to Larry. Avis told me while you were away. He's sick, Ted; he's been home all week and it has to do with his job, somehow."

"What's the matter with him?"

"Avis never talks about their troubles. She must have thought it was important that you know, because she told me to tell you. You're a very special person to Larry."

"I know, I know," he said.

"Maybe you should call, but not about the protests."

"I'll tell her to put him on vitamin C," Margolin said, and felt ugly for having said it and so, had to defend the ugliness, "No wonder he's sick, with all the fuss they make over health and vitamins. Reg, how am *I* supposed to help him? I just got back from *not* helping someone I *liked,* someone I'm 'trained' to help." Her eyebrow rose slightly. "Okay," Margolin went on, "he's naive and I'm jealous of it, but I resent being used as a talent scout for his damn tribes!"

"You don't own primitive man any more than he does." Getting his look, she shrugged. "Well, I've told you about him; you can do what you like," and she left him and went upstairs to oversee the baths.

"Do what I like!" he muttered, and dialed Westercamp's number. He had concocted a vague, neighborly beginning, but when he heard the hope in Avis Westercamp's voice, he knew he wouldn't be able to use it. What did they expect of him? Westercamp got on and Margolin was unprepared for the lowered, pinched quality of the voice; its youthfulness had been conquered, the naive enthusiasm was gone, narrowed to the effort necessary to lift the phone. He was even puffing from the walk. They traded greetings and Margolin found his neck and arms aching with the strain of holding the phone to his ear. He began to throw words into it, needing the sound to listen to. He told Westercamp a wildly doctored story about his visit to three Sioux Indians, and how one had turned out not to be Sioux at all. He tried to make a little joke about the mailing lists. He pushed away heedlessly and the thoughts fled before him into hiding. When he stopped, he was winded.

Westercamp began to speak slowly. "I suppose your wife told you what happened. . . ."

"Not really," he said.

"Trout . . ." Westercamp whispered. Margolin held his breath. "We were developing—uh—resistant to certain—uh—contaminants in the water. I told you."

"I remember," Margolin said.

"We put some in Ede Lake about two months ago. By last week they had died—all of them. And in Swanscombe creek too. The fish could live in foul water"—his newly old voice cracked—"but not in sewers. The river—is a sewer. The lake—is a sewer."

"I know the trout took time to develop——"

"Not the *time,*" Westercamp interrupted querulously. "It's us. We had everything, everything, and we burned it, poisoned it. Why didn't we stop before it was too late? Why can't we stop destroying? Why can't we live *simply,* like the Hunza?"

Margolin caught his breath. The Hunza? New entries in The Noble Savage Sweepstakes.

A student had asked him something before vacation —he should have seen this coming. His old notebook had given:

> The Hunza: small group of Moslem, Subsistence herders, slopes of Himalayas. Close, precarious adaptation to high altitude, short growing season, rugged terrain. (P.8, C.50, IC.6)

The codes indicated the typical Tibetan pattern, but the Utopia-hunters must have been there and come back with the eternal, impossible tales—no anguish, no crime, no locks, men living in vigor to great age. The old dream was blowing into bloom, like a wild poppy. It would be cut back on the edge of fact and lie dormant for a winter only to come bright again some-

where else. Margolin sighed and thought: Your mother
is full of cowboy pictures.

He said gravely into the phone, "Yes, the Hunza."

He could hear Westercamp breathing in his ear, sick
now, and wary of more pain. Suddenly Margolin wanted
to beg his forgiveness; for polluting his air and fouling
his water and for permitting the hideous towers to stand.

Westercamp breathed into the phone again. "People
who have seen them say there are no words for greed
or envy."

"There probably aren't," Margolin said gently.

"They live simply—pure food, good water."

"They are a small, closely knit people," Margolin
added quietly.

". . . and they reverence wisdom. The elders live
to a hundred and twenty." Westercamp's voice had
lightened.

"Moslems," Margolin said, "tend to venerate age."
He was glad when Westercamp missed the point of
this.

"Yes, and wisdom. They don't worship fads, material
things—they're happy, I think, because their lives
are natural. It's good for men to work hard . . ." The
voice had some of its suppleness again. Margolin was
moved. His own torment could never have found
relief in some unknown tribe's good fortune. He knew
that if Utopia existed, he would have envied it, and
not, with Westercamp's singular goodness, wished it
well.

"You see," Westercamp went on, "they're not com-
promised and humiliated all the time. They live as
they should. . . . They don't have to try to convince
everybody of the simplest truths . . . the most obvious
truths."

"A Hunza can understand another Hunza's work,"
Margolin said, "and I think that is a beautiful thing."

"I'm glad you agree. If only we were like them!"

". . . and their language is interesting too," Margolin said, "an old and complex tongue."

When he hung up, he found he had a headache. At three in the morning it was still pounding. The red lights on top of the power-towers were winking on and off, on and off, outside the window.

Margolin sometimes used a hand-made spear-thrower to shock his freshman classes on their first day. He would send the spear into the wall at the back of the class and then, in the sibilant wash of amazement, wade dramatically to his beginning: Primitive Man. . . . At six in the morning Regina traced the strange sound to the basement and found him practicing with the spear-thrower, sending the makeshift spear across the laundry room with terrible savagery. When she asked him what on earth he was throwing it for, he said, breathing hard, "Ninety-three feet, eight inches."

6   Hunting Season

"MAYBE I'LL GO DOWN TO THE creek bank and see if some deers were there last night," he said. The top of his head was level with the counter top where she was working. He put his head all the way back to look up at her, as if she were a sky above him. "Can I, Mommy?"

"Just a minute, will you?" She was measuring flour, and when she had finished and was ready to pay attention to him, his head was still tilted all the way back, because he knew he had to wait and wait for her to get finished with the complicated things she did, and then repeat everything, and even then, half the time it was *no*, anyway. "Now, what was that?" she said.

He asked again.

"All right, you can go, but wear your heavy jacket, because it's getting cold outside."

His heavy jacket wasn't for the cold alone, and they both knew it. It had been made in fear of the Cruel Season. In these bright cold-yellow days, town men put on their talisman clothes, gulped their whiskey, and went up into the hills to hunt and kill. Sometimes they killed one another, and although no hill children had been hurt in many years, it was hard to send them out to play in the sound of the guns.

The little boy was lonely, with all the others in school now. She couldn't keep him indoors, the way some of the other women tried to do—not with everything leading away from their house, trails and tracks and the woods all calling to be explored. So she had made him a little turquoise jacket, unmistakable and in the most unnatural color she could think of.

"Button it up," she said. "I told you it was cold." He began to work the buttons clumsily. Next year he would be going to school; all the kids could walk together down the Notch to be country road. "*To* the creek, not *in* the creek," she told him. "And please, no more smooth stones—we. have a whole basketful already. And if you see any of the hunters on the trail——"

He bore her fussing with stoic patience; his face had the removed look of someone who had already started off, and finally she told him to have a good time, and then he knew he could go. He said good-bye and, yes, he would be back before lunchtime, and he went out into the shivering gold-yellow of the hillside.

She went back into the kitchen, crumbled two cakes of yeast into the potato water she had saved, and started to get the dishes ready to wash. I keep nagging him, she thought. I have such a good eye to peer out and see what he has done wrong once and might do wrong again. . . . She thought about it occasionally, what a shame it was that the boys would never know her as she had been—someone who laughed easily at silly things; who played and didn't care how much it messed up the room; someone who had once liked to stamp windowpanes out of frozen puddles; who had prized laughter, wind, and freedom. Her mind went to the ways she had changed in the years of being a mother. Some of the ways made her a little ashamed.

There was one time when Joseph was trying to tell her about his best friend, Tim. Tim was moving away, and Joseph was shaken with a foretaste of loneliness. There would be nobody to play with on this side of the Notch. She had found herself looking into his ear as he talked, and then going for the small glob of wax with the edge of her apron; then noticing the little crust of sleep at the corner of his eye, and getting that; then straightening his hair—and all the while he was trying to show her his pain, hoping that she could share, from her height, his tragedy—a child's tragedy, written in miniature, told in a small, high voice.

She fussed and fussed and missed the important things. In defense of herself, she knew this was one of the penalties of being a "good" wife and mother. Her life was a mass of details, endless and entangled, all together, all unsorted: trivial things and important things wound into and against one another, all warring for her attention. Changing the goldfish water wasn't vital, but it couldn't wait; teaching the children their Bible was vital, but it could wait. Listening to them, growing with them, that was vital; but the bills had to be paid now, the dinner was burning right now. . . .

She finished with the dishes and went back to the bread, beating the foamed yeast into the well she had made in the flour. Three palmfuls of sugar, one of salt, two eggs. Here it was Friday already, and . . .

Friday! How could she have let him go out today? She put down the bread paddle at the edge of the bowl, where it fell over into the dough and sank. Friday. Had the week gone so fast? He had been on his new medicine since last Friday. His last seizure had been on Friday. They had gone down-mountain to the doctor, and the doctor had changed the medicine again.

"Don't worry about your little boy," he had said. "We'll get control of the seizures; it will take time, that's all." He had given her medication for two weeks. "And if he has no trouble with it, you can just call the office, and I'll have it made up for him, the way we did it before."

She had had to tell him humbly that she didn't like to use the phone to call him because of the party line.

"Maybe it's a good idea not to, then," he had said gently. "It wouldn't do to put a stigma on him. We're going to get him under control before he starts to school, and then nobody need know. Until we find the right combination of medicine—something that gives control without getting him too groggy—well, there are going to be problems." Then the doctor had got up, his way of ending their conversation. "The difficulty will be for you, not for him. You can be grateful that epilepsy is most merciful to the people who have it—he's not conscious of his seizures, doesn't know he has them. The loss of all the time he's out—that might puzzle him; that, and your attitude, perhaps. But—you just let *me* worry. In every other way, he's a fine, healthy boy."

One week and no seizure, though she had waited, half wanting it to come and be over, fearful of a vain hope that his medicine might be right at last. Every evening when Cal came home, his eyes asking, "Did it happen?" and her eyes answering, "Not today" went before all other greetings, questions, news, kiss at the door.

Now it was Friday again, and he had never gone longer than a week without a seizure. Now he was walking up over Pickax Hill, past the old mine and then down the steep gully, all rock. Guns would be going off over his head and frightened animals bursting the thickets to outrun their panic. Death would be all around him. He was sure to stop at the creek, enchanted with the round stones, bending down to play with them and watch the water go over; he would be bending over the shocking chill water. . . .

She couldn't stop seeing her Mother-Pictures—how a seizure could catch him at the top of the hill, no warning. He could fall, thrashing, unable to breathe, his face going gray for lack of air, and then down the rocky gully, falling, and there was the water. He would be in the water while the paroxysms slowed and the unconsciousness began. How could he begin to breathe again, with his head in the water? (Always the first infinitesimal breath after a seizure had been a miracle to her. It was a promise that the next breath would come, and the next, each one a little longer, until Breath itself had been given back to him, and slowly, slowly, his life.) It was an awful picture, the water holding him so that his breath could never again promise. . . .

She shook herself free of the picture, but it didn't leave her. It stayed, brimming the edges of her mind, ready to flow back when she relaxed her vigil against it. "He had his medicine this morning," she said to the empty house. "He looked fine when he went out."

Of course he looked fine. Didn't the seizures catch him in the middle of a word, a step, a thought across his mind? He might be in the midst of running: leg up, arm out, his face eager with success. Motion would be frozen, and then a cry squandering all his breath. Then he would fall into the rhythmic spasms that conquered everything, and an eternity without breathing. It took only a second for the happy, healthy boy to disappear. Now he was going up Pickax Hill, up near the old mine, the sudden hunters, the gully, the rocks, the water.

"I can't stay here any more!" she said to the house. She pulled her old work jacket off the hook and ran out the door.

For a single eye-struck moment she forgot what had brought her outside. She stood still, gasping with the beauty of the sunlight that was still slanting from the east, catching itself in the hillside's trees, its golden light pouring through a million translucent screens of veined paper. The colors trembled and vibrated with the light, but the leaf sound was brittle in the wind, like a scattering applause of old people, dry and hesitant. Above the feverish trees there was a sky cut clean by the sharp edge of a harder wind.

She followed the little path and crossed the Notch. After that, there were only deer trails up the near side of Pickax Hill. The mines and roads were over the summit. How she hated and feared those old mine shafts! These hills were full of raped land the takers had plundered and left unhealed. Mines and quarries still poured yellow trailings from their wounds. She heard a gun, then another. Now the hunters too. A world of rape and murder, a whole world. Her head ached with the horror of all the possibilities. She had to find him and stop the pictures in her head.

The shimmering golden forest moved in upon the trail. Where was the little turquoise jacket? Ahead of her, the way wound and sought upward, hidden by trees and brush. Where was he? Could he have gone so far? She nosed the wind like an animal. Was that he, calling? Was that his cry? She began to run listening, smelling the air for danger. And then she saw, on the trail ahead of her, the turquoise jacket going up and down with his steps as he marched along. She cut over and off into the woods, keeping behind him, tracking. I mustn't let him see me, she thought. He doesn't know what he has, what takes him and transforms him. She could see his face as he said, "Everybody else goes up the hill and down to the creek. You don't think I'm big enough! You think I'm a *baby*!" Oh, that worst of all insults!

She kept uphill of him and behind the beacon

jacket, tracking him warily, stopping when she got too close, not daring to let her breath sob out on a wind that might carry the sound to him. It was hard not to pant for breath. She thought: When did I get so old and fat—a middle-aged huntress in a ratty apron, puffing uphill with the grace of a runaway tractor?

He put his head up, reading the air for something, and she crouched lower.

For a while, he dawdled over a fork in the trail, and she watched from her cover, seething against him. (Why do you tell me you are going to go someplace and then turn right around and go someplace else instead! What if I had to look for you one day, when you'd told me, oh, the creek, and it wasn't the creek you had gone to, but the canyon? Don't you know that you could be lost or finished in a moment? Don't you know that you are a miracle, and irreplaceable— you stupid, stupid boy!) Below her, he made up his mind idly and turned uptrail again, and she followed him, tracking.

They skirted the summit, leveled, and started over toward the south. The scattered heaps of tailings from the mines began. They lay spewed from the openings of shafts or drill holes, and the water that they leached turned acid and killed the plants it touched.

Over to the north, she heard the guns of the hunters. The boy crossed again and started down toward the sound of the guns, cutting obliquely down the north side to where the creek ran. She backtracked and came up again at his left, being careful not to stumble, not to make noise in the leaves that lay blown in heaps for the afternoon schoolboys to play in. When she came up again, she didn't see him. The panic and pictures flooded back. She went to the brow of the hill, tracking.

She kept away from the top, where they had been, and looked out toward the north and east. The downward slope was more gentle there; there were fewer rocks, and the creek flowed almost level and had laid banks of soft, alluvial sand for itself on either side.

He was standing close to the bank, immediately below her, looking across the creek and picking his nose intently. In the midst of her relief, her hand came up in the gesture that had become automatic to her—and her mouth opened to say, "Don't do that." She thought suddenly: I'm not saving him, I'm saving myself. I'm not even looking out for him—I'm *spying*. What am I doing here, invading his pitiful little private time?

He stood very small and straight against all the land and sky that reached around her. His back was to her, and his ears stuck out so bravely, and his neck was set bravely on his thin shoulders. What if it wasn't a seizure now, but a wasp stinging him—wouldn't she run down to the bank to comfort him? When the creek bed froze, he would want to skate with the other boys on the pond downstream, to go sled riding, howling down the hillsides in his joyfear. What if he should be thrown over in the snow, hit a tree, hit a rock? Could she follow him everywhere to pick him up? Weren't there tunnels in the mine?

Over north, the shooting started up again.

He was standing on the bank, sifting sand through his fingers, and he began to talk in his high, clear voice—his own thoughts, which she was not meant to hear. "Listen, you rocks over there—you better shape up! You're not so tough, you big, damn rocks! My brothers go to school. When I go to school, I'm going to learn all about *you*, but you will never know about *me*, and you will be in my power." Then he shouted at them, *"Do you hear me?"* It was her intonation exactly, all the querulous anger of her impatience and all the long-suffering in her tone, captured with unconscious, searing honesty.

It was his world of rape and murder, too—he had to make it his.

"Yes, I hear you," she whispered, and turned and walked back down the hill.

7   And Sarah Laughed

SHE WENT TO THE WINDOW EVERY fifteen minutes to see if they were coming. They would be taking the new highway cutoff; it would bring them past the south side of the farm; past the unused, dilapidated outbuildings instead of the orchards and fields that were now full and green. It would look like a poor place to the new bride. Her first impression of their farm would be of age and bleached-out, dried-out buildings on which the doors hung open like a row of gaping mouths that said nothing.

All day, Sarah had gone about her work clumsy with eagerness and hesitant with dread, picking up utensils to forget them in holding, finding them two minutes later a surprise in her hand. She had been planning and working ever since Abel wrote to them from Chicago that he was coming home with a wife. Everything should have been clean and orderly. She wanted the bride to know as soon as she walked inside what kind of woman Abel's mother was—to feel, without a word having to be said, the house's dignity, honesty, simplicity, and love. But the spring cleaning had been late, and Alma Yoder had gotten sick—Sarah had had to go over to the Yoders and help out.

Now she looked around and saw that it was no use trying to have everything ready in time. Abel and his bride would be coming any minute. If she didn't want to get caught shedding tears of frustration, she'd better get herself under control. She stepped over the pile of clothes still unsorted for the laundry and went out on the back porch.

The sky was blue and silent, but as she watched, a bird passed over the fields crying. The garden spread out before her, displaying its varying greens. Beyond it, along the creek, there was a row of poplars. It always calmed her to look at them. She looked today. She and Matthew had planted those trees. They stood thirty feet high now, stately as figures in a procession. Once —only once and many years ago—she had tried to describe in words the sounds that the wind made as it combed those trees on its way west. The little boy to whom she had spoken was a grown man now, and he was bringing home a wife. *Married. . . .*

Ever since he had written to tell them he was coming with his bride, Sarah had been going back in her mind to the days when she and Matthew were bride and groom and then mother and father. Until now, it hadn't seemed so long ago. Her life had flowed on past her, blurring the early days with Matthew when this farm was strange and new to her and when the silence of it was sharp and bitter like pain, not dulled and familiar like an echo of old age.

Matthew hadn't changed much. He was a tall, lean man, but he had had a boy's spareness then. She remembered how his smile came, wavered and went uncertainly, but how his eyes had never left her. He followed everything with his eyes. Matthew had always been a silent man; his face was expressionless and his body stiff with reticence, but his eyes had sought her out eagerly and held her and she had been warm in his look.

Sarah and Matthew had always known each other —their families had been neighbors. Sarah was a plain girl, a serious "decent" girl. Not many of the young men asked her out, and when Matthew did and did again, her parents had been pleased. Her father told her that Matthew was a good man, as steady as any woman could want. He came from honest, hard-working people and he would prosper any farm he had. Her mother spoke shyly of how his eyes woke when Sarah came into the room, and how they followed her. If she married him, her life would be full of the things she knew and loved, an easy, familiar world with her parents' farm not two miles down the road. But no one wanted to mention the one thing that worried Sarah: the fact that Matthew was deaf. It was what stopped her from saying yes right away; she loved him, but she was worried about his deafness. The things she feared about it were the practical things: a fall or a fire when he wouldn't hear her cry for help. Only long after she had put those fears aside and moved the scant two miles into his different world, did she realize that the things she had feared were the wrong things.

Now they had been married for twenty-five years. It was a good marriage—good enough. Matthew was generous, strong, and loving. The farm prospered. His silence made him seem more patient, and because she became more silent also, their neighbors saw in them the dignity and strength of two people who do not rail against misfortune, who were beyond trivial talk and gossip; whose lives needed no words. Over the years of help given and meetings attended, people noticed how little they needed to say. Only Sarah's friend Luita knew that in the beginning, when they were first married, they had written yearning notes to each other. But Luita didn't know that the notes also were mute.

Sarah had never shown them to anyone, although she kept them all, and sometimes she would go up and get the box out of her closet and read them over. She had saved every scrap, from questions about the eggs to the tattered note he had left beside his plate on their first anniversary. He had written it when she was busy at the stove and then he'd gone out and she hadn't seen it until she cleared the table.

The note said: "I love you derest wife Sarah. I pray you have happy day all day your life."

When she wanted to tell him something, she spoke to him slowly, facing him, and he took the words as they formed on her lips. His speaking voice was thick and hard to understand and he perceived that it was unpleasant. He didn't like to use it. When he had to say something, he used his odd, grunting tone, and she came to understand what he said. If she ever hungered for laughter from him or the little meaningless talk that confirms existence and affection, she told herself angrily that Matthew talked through his work. Words die in the air; they can be turned one way or another, but Matthew's work prayed and laughed for him. He took good care of her and the boys, and they idolized him. Surely that counted more than all the words— words that meant and didn't mean—behind which people could hide.

Over the years she seldom noticed her own increasing silence, and there were times when his tenderness, which was always given without words, seemed to her to make his silence beautiful.

She thought of the morning she had come downstairs feeling heavy and off balance with her first pregnancy—with Abel. She had gone to the kitchen to begin the day, taking the coffeepot down and beginning to fill it when her eye caught something on the kitchen table. For a minute she looked around in confusion. They had already laid away what the baby would need:

diapers, little shirts and bedding, all folded away in the
drawer upstairs, but here on the table was a bounty
of cloth, all planned and scrimped for and bought
from careful, careful study of the catalogue—yards of
patterned flannel and plissé, coat wool and bright red
corduroy. Sixteen yards of yellow ribbon for bindings.
Under the coat wool was cloth Matthew had chosen for
her; blue with a little gray figure. It was silk, and there
was a card on which was rolled precisely enough lace
edging for her collar and sleeves. All the long studying
and careful planning, all in silence.

She had run upstairs and thanked him and hugged
him, but it was no use showing delight with words,
making plans, matching cloth and figuring which
pieces would be for the jacket and which for sleepers. Most wives used such fussing to tell their husbands
how much they thought of their gifts. But Matthew's
silence was her silence too.

When he had left to go to the orchard after breakfast
that morning, she had gone to their room and stuffed
her ears with cotton, trying to understand the world as
it must be to him, with no sound. The cotton dulled
the outside noises a little, but it only magnified all the
noises in her head. Scratching her cheek caused a roar
like a downpour of rain; her own voice was like
thunder. She knew Matthew could not hear his own
voice in his head. She could not be deaf as he was deaf.
She could not know such silence ever.

So she found herself talking to the baby inside her,
telling it the things she would have told Matthew, the
idle daily things: Didn't Margaret Amson look peaked
in town? Wasn't it a shame the drugstore had
stopped stocking lump alum—her pickles wouldn't be
the same.

Abel was a good baby. He had Matthew's great
eyes and gentle ways. She chattered to him all day,

looking forward to his growing up, when there would be confidences between them. She looked to the time when he would have his own picture of the world, and with that keen hunger and hope she had a kind of late blooming into a beauty that made people in town turn to look at her when she passed in the street holding the baby in the fine clothes she had made for him. She took Abel everywhere, and came to know a pride that was very new to her, a plain girl from a modest family who had married a neighbor boy. When they went to town, they always stopped over to see Matthew's parents and her mother.

Mama had moved to town after Pa died. Of course they had offered to have Mama come and live with them, but Sarah was glad she had gone to a little place in town, living where there were people she knew and things happening right outside her door. Sarah remembered them visiting on a certain spring day, all sitting in Mama's new front room. They sat uncomfortably in the genteel chairs, and Abel crawled around on the floor as the women talked, looking up every now and then for his father's nod of approval. After a while he went to catch the sunlight that was glancing off a crystal nut dish and scattering rainbow bands on the floor. Sarah smiled down at him. She too had a radiance, and, for the first time in her life, she knew it. She was wearing the dress she had made from Matthew's cloth —it became her and she knew that too, so she gave her joy freely as she traded news with Mama.

Suddenly they heard the fire bell ringing up on the hill. She caught Matthew's eye and mouthed, "Fire engines," pointing uphill to the firehouse. He nodded.

In the next minutes there was the strident, off-key blare as every single one of Arcadia's volunteer firemen —his car horn plugged with a matchstick and his duty before him—drove hellbent for the firehouse in an ecstasy of bell and siren. In a minute the ding-ding-

ding-ding careened in deafening, happy privilege through every red light in town.

"Big bunch of boys!" Mama laughed. "You can count two Saturdays in good weather when they don't have a fire, and that's during the hunting season!"

They laughed. Then Sarah looked down at Abel, who was still trying to catch the wonderful colors. A madhouse of bells, horns, screaming sirens had gone right past them and he hadn't cried, he hadn't looked, he hadn't turned. Sarah twisted her head sharply away and screamed to the china cats on the whatnot shelf as loud as she could, but Abel's eyes only flickered to the movement and then went back to the sun and its colors.

Mama whispered, "Oh, my dear God!"

Sarah began to cry bitterly, uncontrollably, while her husband and son looked on, confused, embarrassed, unknowing.

The silence drew itself over the seasons and the seasons layered into years. Abel was a good boy; Matthew was a good man.

Later, Rutherford, Lindsay, and Franklin Delano came. They too were silent. Hereditary nerve deafness was rare, the doctors all said. The boys might marry and produce deaf children, but it was not likely. When they started to school, the administrators and teachers told her that the boys would be taught specially to read lips and to speak. They would not be "abnormal," she was told. Nothing would show their handicap, and with training no one need know that they were deaf. But the boys seldom used their lifeless voices to call to their friends; they seldom joined games unless they were forced to join. No one but their mother understood their speech. No teacher could stop all the jumping, turning, gum-chewing schoolboys, or remember herself to face front from the blackboard to the sound-closed boys. The lip-reading exercises never seemed to make plain differences—"man," "pan," "began."

But the boys had work and pride in the farm. The seasons varied their silence with colors—crows flocked in the snowy fields in winter, and tones of golden wheat darkened across acres of summer wind. If the boys couldn't hear the bedsheets flapping on the wash-line, they could see and feel the autumn day. There were chores and holidays and the wheel of birth and planting, hunting, fishing, and harvest. The boys were familiar in town; nobody ever laughed at them, and when Sarah met neighbors at the store, they praised her sons with exaggerated praise, well meant, saying that no one could tell, no one could really tell unless they knew, about the boys not hearing.

Sarah wanted to cry to these kindly women that the simple orders the boys obeyed by reading her lips were not a miracle. If she could ever hear in their long-practiced robot voices a question that had to do with feelings and not facts, and answer it in words that rose beyond the daily, tangible things done or not done, *that* would be a miracle.

Her neighbors didn't know that they themselves con-fided to one another from a universe of hopes, a world they wanted half lost in the world that was; how often they spoke pitting inflection against meaning to soften it, harden it, make a joke of it, curse by it, bless by it. They didn't realize how they wrapped the bare words of love in gentle humor or wild insults that the loved ones knew were ways of keeping the secret of love between the speaker and the hearer. Mothers lovingly called their children crow-bait, mouse-meat, devils. They predicted dark ends for them, and the children heard the secrets beneath the words, heard them and smiled and knew, and let the love said-unsaid caress their souls. With her own bitter knowledge Sarah could only thank them for well-meaning and return to silence.

Standing on the back porch now, Sarah heard the wind in the poplars and she sighed. It was getting on to noon. Warm air was beginning to ripple the fields. Matthew would be ready for lunch soon, but she wished she could stand out under the warm sky forever and listen to birds stitching sounds into the endless silence. She found herself thinking about Abel again, and the bride. She wondered what Janice would be like. Abel had gone all the way to Chicago to be trained in drafting. He had met her there, in the school. Sarah was afraid of a girl like that. They had been married quickly, without family or friends or toasts or gifts or questions. It hinted at some kind of secret shame. It frightened her. That kind of girl was independent and she might be scornful of a dowdy mother-in-law. And the house was still a mess.

From down the road, dust was rising. Matthew must have seen it too. He came over the rise and toward the house walking faster than usual. He'd want to slick his hair down and wash up to meet the stranger his son had become. She ran inside and bundled up the unsorted laundry, ran upstairs and pulled a comb through her hair, put on a crooked dab of lipstick, banged her shin, took off her apron and saw a spot on her dress, put the apron on again and shouted a curse to all the disorder she suddenly saw around her.

Now the car was crunching up the thin gravel of the driveway. She heard Matthew downstairs washing up, not realizing that the bride and groom were already at the house. Protect your own, she thought, and ran down to tell him. Together they went to the door and opened it, hoping that at least Abel's familiar face would comfort them.

They didn't recognize him at first, and he didn't see them. He and the tiny bride might have been alone in the world. He was walking around to open the door for her, helping her out, bringing her up the path to the house, and all the time their fingers and hands moved and spun meanings at which they smiled and laughed; they were talking somehow, painting thoughts in the air so fast with their fingers that Sarah couldn't see where one began and the other ended. She stared. The school people had always told her that such finger-talk set the deaf apart. It was abnormal; it made freaks of them. . . . How soon Abel had accepted someone else's strangeness and bad ways. She felt so dizzy she thought she was going to fall, and she was more bitterly jealous than she had ever been before.

The little bride stopped before them appealingly and in her dead, deaf-rote voice, said, "Ah-am pliizd to meet'ou." Sarah put out her hand dumbly and it was taken and the girl's eyes shone. Matthew smiled, and this time the girl spoke and waved her hands in time to her words, and then gave Matthew her hand. So Abel had told that girl about Matthew's deafness. It had never been a secret, but Sarah felt somehow be-trayed.

They had lunch, saw the farm, the other boys came home from their summer school and met Janice. Sarah put out cake and tea and showed Abel and Janice up to the room she had made ready for them, and all the time the two of them went on with love-talk in their fingers; the jokes and secrets knitted silently between them, fears told and calmed, hopes spoken and echoed in the silence of a kitchen where twenty-five years of silence had imprisoned her. Always they would stop and pull themselves back to their good manners, speaking or writing polite questions and answers for the family; but in a moment or two, the talk would flag, the urgent hunger would overcome them and they would fight it, resolutely turning their eyes to Sarah's mouth. Then the signs would creep into their fingers, and the joy of talk into their faces, and they would fall before the conquering need of their communion.

Sarah's friend Luita came the next day, in the afternoon. They sat over tea with the kitchen window open for the cool breeze and Sarah was relieved and grateful to hold to a familiar thing now that her life had suddenly become so strange to her. Luita hadn't changed at all, thank God—not the hand that waved her tea cool or the high giggle that broke into generous laughter.

"She's darling!" Luita said after Janice had been introduced, and, thankfully, had left them. Sarah didn't want to talk about her, so she agreed without enthusiasm.

Luita only smiled back. "Sarah, you'll never pass for pleased with a face like that."

"It's just—just her ways," Sarah said. "She never even wrote to us before the wedding, and now she comes in and—and changes everything. I'll be honest, Luita, I didn't want Abel to marry someone who was deaf. What did we train him for, all those special classes? . . . *not* to marry another deaf person. And she hangs on him like a wood tick all day . . ." She didn't mention the signs. She couldn't.

Luita said, "It's just somebody new in the house, that's all. She's important to you, but a stranger. Addie Purkhard felt the same way and you know what a lovely girl Velma turned out to be. It just took time. . . . She's going to have a baby, did she tell you?"

"Baby? Who?" Sarah cried, feeling cold and terrified.

"Why, *Velma*. A baby due about a month after my Dolores'."

It had never occurred to Sarah that Janice and Abel could have a baby. She wanted to stop thinking about it and she looked back at Luita whose eyes were glowing with something joyful that had to be said. Luita hadn't been able to see beyond it to the anguish of her friend.

Luita said, "You know, Sarah, things haven't been

so good between Sam and me. . . ." She cleared her throat. "You know how stubborn he is. The last few weeks, it's been like a whole new start for us. I came over to tell you about it because I'm so happy, and I had to share it with you."

She looked away shyly, and Sarah pulled herself together and leaned forward, putting her hand on her friend's arm. "I'm so happy for you. What happened?"

"It started about three weeks ago—a night that neither of us could get to sleep. We hadn't been arguing; there was just that awful coldness, as if we'd both been frozen stiff. One of us started talking—just lying there in the dark. I don't even know who started, but pretty soon we were telling each other the most secret things—things we never could have said in the light. He finally told me that Dolores having a baby makes him feel old and scared. He's afraid of it, Sarah, and I never knew it, and it explains why he hates to go over and see them, and why he argues with Ken all the time. Right there beside me he told me so many things I'd forgotten or misunderstood. In the dark it's like thinking out loud—like being alone and yet together at the same time. I love him so and I came so close to forgetting it. . . ."

Sarah lay in bed and thought about Luita and Sam sharing their secrets in the dark. Maybe even now they were talking in their flower-papered upstairs room, moving against the engulfing seas of silence as if in little boats, finding each other and touching and then looking out in awe at the vastness all around them where they might have rowed alone and mute forever. She wondered if Janice and Abel fingered those signs in the dark on each other's body. She began to cry. There was that freedom, at least; other wives had to strangle their weeping.

When she was cried out, she lay in bed and counted

all the good things she had: children, possessions, acres of land, respect of neighbors, the years of certainty and success. Then she conjured the little bride, and saw her standing in front of Abel's old car as she had at first —with nothing; all her virtues still unproven, all her fears still forming, and her bed in another woman's house. Against the new gold ring on the bride's finger, Sarah threw all the substance of her years to weigh for her. The balance went with the bride. It wasn't fair! The balance went with the bride because she had put that communion in the scales as well, and all the thoughts that must have been given and taken between them. It outweighed Sarah's twenty-five years of muteness; outweighed the house and barn and well-tended land, and the sleeping family keeping their silent thoughts.

The days went by. Sarah tortured herself with elaborate courtesy to Janice and politeness to the accomplice son, but she couldn't guard her own envy from herself and she found fault wherever she looked. Now the silence of her house was throbbing with her anger. Every morning Janice would come and ask to help, but Sarah was too restless to teach her, so Janice would sit for a while waiting and then get up and go outside to look for Abel. Then Sarah would decide to make coleslaw and sit with the chopping bowl in her lap, smashing the chopper against the wood with a vindictive joy that she alone could hear the sounds she was making, that she alone knew how savage they were and how satisfying.

At church she would see the younger boys all clean and handsome, Matthew greeting friends, Janice demure and fragile, and Abel proud and loving, and she would feel a terrible guilt for her unreasonable anger; but back from town afterwards, and after Sunday dinner, she noticed as never before how disheveled the boys looked, how ugly their hollow voices sounded. Had Matthew always been so patient and unruffled? He was like one of his own stock, an animal, a dumb animal.

Janice kept asking to help and Sarah kept saying there wasn't time to teach her. She was amazed when Matthew, who was very fussy about his fruit, suggested to her that Janice might be able to take care of the grapes and, later, work in the orchard.

"I haven't time to teach her!"

"Ah owill teeech Ja-nuss," Abel said, and they left right after dinner in too much of a hurry.

Matthew stopped Sarah when she was clearing the table and asked why she didn't like Janice. Now it was Sarah's turn to be silent, and when Matthew insisted, Sarah finally turned on him. "You don't understand," she shouted. "You don't understand a thing!" And she saw on his face the same look of confusion she had seen that day in Mama's fussy front room when she had suddenly begun to cry and could not stop. She turned away with the plates, but suddenly his hand shot out and he struck them to the floor, and the voice he couldn't hear or control rose to an awful cry, "Ah ahm dehf! Ah ahm dehf!" Then he went out, slamming the door without the satisfaction of its sound.

If a leaf fell or a stalk sprouted in the grape arbor, Janice told it over like a set of prayers. One night at supper, Sarah saw the younger boys framing those dumb-signs of hers, and she took them outside and slapped their hands. "*We* don't do that!" she shouted at them, and to Janice later she said, "Those . . . signs you make—I know they must have taught you to do that, but out here . . . well, it isn't our way."

Janice looked back at her in a confusion for which there were no words.

It was no use raging at Janice. Before she had come

there had never been anything for Sarah to be angry about. . . . What did they all exepct of her? Wasn't it enough that she was left out of a world that heard and laughed without being humiliated by the love-madness they made with their hands? It was like watching them undressing.

The wind cannot be caught. Poplars may sift it, a rising bird can breast it, but it will pass by and no one can stop it. She saw the boys coming home at a dead run now, and they couldn't keep their hands from taking letters, words, and pictures from the fingers of the lovers. If they saw an eagle, caught a fish, or got scolded, they ran to their brother or his wife, and Sarah had to stand in the background and demand to be told.

One day Matthew came up to her and smiled and said, "Look." He put out his two index fingers and hooked the right down on the left, then the left down gently on the right. "Fwren," he said, "Ja-nuss say, fwren."

To Sarah there was something obscene about all those gestures, and she said, "I don't like people waving their hands around like monkeys in a zoo!" She said it very clearly so that he couldn't mistake it.

He shook his head violently and gestured as he spoke. "Mouth eat; mouth kiss, mouth tawk! Fin-ger wohk; fin-ger tawk. E-ah" (and he grabbed his ear, violently), "e-ah dehf. *Mihn*," (and he rapped his head, violently, as if turning a terrible impatience against himself so as to spare her) "*mihn not* dehf!"

Later she went to the barn after something and she ran into Lindsay and Franklin Delano standing guilt-ily, and when she caught them in her eye as she turned, she saw their hands framing signs. They didn't come into the house until it was nearly dark. Was their hunger for those signs so great that only darkness could bring them home? They weren't bad boys, the kind who would do a thing just because you told them not to. Did their days have a hunger too, or was it only the spell of the lovers, honey-honeying to shut out a world of moving mouths and silence?

At supper she looked around the table and was re-assured. It could have been any farm family sitting there, respectable and quiet. A glance from the father was all that was needed to keep order or summon another helping. Their eyes were lowered, their faces composed. The hands were quiet. She smiled and went to the kitchen to fix the shortcake she had made as a surprise.

When she came back, they did not notice her immediately. They were all busy talking. Janice was telling them something and they all had their mouths ridiculously pursed with the word. Janice smiled in assent and each one showed her his sign and she smiled at each one and nodded, and the signers turned to one another in their joy, accepting and begging acceptance. Then they saw Sarah standing there; the hands came down, the faces faded.

She took the dinner plates away and brought in the dessert things, and when she went back to the kitchen for the cake, she began to cry. It was beyond envy now; it was too late for measuring or weighing. She had lost. In the country of the blind, Mama used to say, the one-eyed man is king. Having been a citizen of such a country, she knew better. In the country of the deaf, the hearing man is lonely. Into that country a girl had come who, with a wave of her hand, had given the deaf ears for one another, and had made Sarah the deaf one.

Sarah stood, staring at her cake and feeling for that moment the profundity of the silence which she had once tried to match by stuffing cotton in her ears. Everyone she loved was in the other room, talking, sharing, standing before the awful, impersonal heaven and the unhearing earth with pictures of his thoughts, and she was the deaf one now. It wasn't "any farm family," silent in its strength. It was a yearning family, silent in its hunger, and a demure little bride had shown them all how deep the hunger was. She had shown Sarah that her youth had been sold into silence. She was too old to change now.

An anger rose in her as she stared at the cake. Why should they be free to move and gesture and look different while she was kept in bondage to their silence? Then she remembered Matthew's mute notes, his pride in Abel's training, his face when he had cried, "I am deaf!" over and over. She had actually fought that terrible yearning, that hunger they all must have had for their own words. If they could all speak somehow, what would the boys tell her?

She knew what she wanted to tell them. That the wind sounds through the poplar trees, and people have a hard time speaking to one another even if they aren't deaf. Luita and Sam had to have a night to hide their faces while they spoke. It suddenly occurred to her that if Matthew made one of those signs with his hands and she could learn that sign, she could put her hands against his in the darkness, and read the meaning—that if she learned those signs she could hear him. . . .

She dried her eyes hurriedly and took in the cake. They saw her and the hands stopped, drooping lifelessly again; the faces waited mutely. Silence. It was a silence she could no longer bear. She looked from face to face. What was behind those eyes she loved? Didn't everyone's world go deeper than chores and bread and sleep?

"I want to talk to you," she said. "I want to talk, to know what you think." She put her hands out before her, offering them.

Six pairs of eyes watched her.

Janice said, "Mo-ther."

Eyes snapped away to Janice; thumb was under lip: the Sign.

Sarah followed them. "Wife," she said, showing her ring.

"Wife," Janice echoed, thumb under lip to the clasp of hands.

Sarah said, "I love. . . ."

Janice showed her and she followed hesitantly and then turned to Matthew to give and to be received in that sign.

8   To the Members
of the D.A.R.

THERE WERE LETTERS: *To the Members of the D.A.R., To the American Camera Club, To the International Brotherhood of Trainmen, To the alumni of the Eastman School of Music. When they all met at Heron Landing at three o'clock on the sixteenth of May, as per instruction, all bright-flowered dresses and bandoliered with cameras (ready for the Convention, the Tryouts, the Concert), they looked, each of them, for one of his own kind.*

She looked for choral singers, and wondered who the other people could be. The social distinctions drawn from preference are unmistakable, ". . . and this is not an a capella *crowd*," she told her husband.

He looked at the milling, waiting group, bright against the gray, ramshackled landing, and had to agree.

She turned to the woman beside her. "I'm looking forward to Lassus and Byrd," she said, testing.

The woman, testing, smiled. "Are you a Daughter?"

Then they both said, "I beg your pardon?"

He, to a man: "Eastman Singers?"

The man, to him: "Eastman Kodak Camera club."

Their bright clothes began to boil: turning, submerging and rising again, moving to ask, to answer, to ask. Then someone shouted from the center of the turning, "We've been tricked, fooled, brought out to this godforsaken place! It's some kind of trick!" Then the crowd turned outward from itself to seek the reason there. It was too late. They were surrounded by the stolid, uniformed men and the simple, unequivocal horror of the guns. . . .

She screamed.

"What is it?" Martin cried, shocked from sleep.

"What is it?" the two old people cried, running along the hall to their daughter's room.

"She's had a nightmare, that's all." Martin took his wife in his arms and comforted her, and the two old people looked away, unconvinced of his power to comfort and saddened by their own helplessness. They went back to their room unconvinced and tried to sleep again.

"It was awful," Julia said. "It was weird, but something made it seem so real. . . ."

He smoothed the covers over her and got into bed. "It's all right," he said. "It was just a dream."

In the morning there were all the calls to make to relatives, and new apologies to Julia's parents for having left the kids at home this time. Her parents didn't seem to be moved by the relentlessness of the apologies; they didn't realize how relentless their questions were. Julia was inside on the phone and Martin could hear her answering the same questions with the same apologies.

"Does Julia always have such horrible dreams?" Mrs. Spiro asked.

Martin found himself defensive and said "Of course

not," which made it seem as if they or their house were at fault, and so he had to exculpate everyone again: It was the trip, the excitement, and so on, and so on. . . . They didn't believe him; he could see it. Their Nicholas had married and gone away with his vulgar wife and never came to visit unless he was called. Their George had gone away with his stupid wife and never came to them unless he was called, and this one had taken their Julia a thousand miles away and they came in only once a year and hurried back as from a plague.

Martin remembered that in the vacation atmosphere of the plane he had planned to do something worthwhile along with their visit to Julia's parents. There were some fine Speech Therapy Departments in this city. He had thought he might stop by some of them to talk shop and see if any special work was being done. He knew now that he would have to stay with Julia, who was tied to the house, the phone, apologies, and excuses. He had to defend her every minute, and in the end, to defend himself.

"They are our grandchildren," Mr. Spiro complained, as the evening echoed the morning, "yet if we saw them on the street, we wouldn't recognize them."

"Oh, I don't think——"

"Yet, I suppose you have reasons——"

Martin was feeling raw and sensitive after his day of defending. "We've never had much time to ourselves. My work is demanding, and Julia is always home with the kids."

"I suppose when people are young," Mr. Spiro said, gliding past the answer as if it had been inaudible, "they think less of duty and more of pleasure."

Martin held that description up against his life and failed to see any similarity between it and the old house he and his family lived in, money problems, the kids' mumps and measles, his patients, and Julia's tired evening face. There was from that world, however, nothing to declare.

Mr. Spiro began to sound on another tightened string. "These insane people you work with—you say it is demanding work—"

"My patients aren't mentally ill," Martin explained, as he had explained on each yearly visit for all the seven years of his marriage. "Some of them are stroke victims; some have brain damage which gives them aphasia. They have to learn to speak again. I help them learn."

"You have explained this before," Mr. Spiro said a little peevishly. "I did not understand it then. I do not understand it now. What sort of work is this for a man to do?"

Martin felt the string snapping. The man didn't know aphasia from Eurasia, but he knew where the fret on that string was and how to give it the breaking twist. It was an amazing, clear vision, a gift with him, a talent. He couldn't *know* that most speech therapists were women, and that the pay of a speech therapist was woman's pay. The part that hurt, of course, had to do with the way he felt about keeping Julia in a house she hated. It was an old house, but it was all they could afford. It meant poverty to her, a feeling that nothing could really help them, that they were defeated by the job Martin loved. She hadn't complained about it lately, but now, in his father-in-law's house, he was reminded of it. He began talking about an interesting case. He talked to keep from thinking until Julia and her mother finished the dishes.

They rode in small motor skiffs through labyrinthine swamps festooned with moss and vines and rank with living things and dead. Snakes peered at them with clinical eyes and undulated away to wait in tussocks of coarse grass. Crocodiles rose and sank with deliberate silence. Bubbles and oily scum glazed the fermenting water, and the prisoners gasped for breath. Terror had changed all of them. Their ruddy faces were already sallow, their bright clothes already gray. She stood close to him in the boat, but she felt alone, ashamed of him for being helpless, of herself for having been the cause of it. In the middle of a pond of gray water the boats stopped, and while the guards stared impassively, one boatman poled over to a large dead tree sticking out of the water. He opened some sort of door cut into the tree and reached inside. There was a buzzing sound and a huge grid lifted out of the water. The boats started up again and the grid fell back after them. "Electrified," the guard said; "five thousand volts. . . . Won't be long now—we're almost there."

When they reached the Island, it was almost dark. They were marched to rows of barracks—the men to one, women to another, children to a third. No one went out. Some slept out their exhaustion and dreamed; some stayed awake and wept with fear or rage.

"First few nights," the guards said. "After that, they don't have the strength."

"Julia!" Martin turned on the light. "I heard you moaning. . . . Are you all right?"

"Dream . . ." she said, and struggled to free the swamp from her eyes and hair.

"Are you all right?"

She looked around the room for any shreds of the mossy trees that might still be hanging from the walls, or for an empty alligator skin draped over the chair like a discarded costume.

"Julia. . .?"

"Just a bad dream," she said. "I'm okay now. Turn

the light out. We don't want to disturb them." Her eyes turned to where her parents lay beyond the wall. She was sure that Martin wanted to ask her if it was the same one she had had last night. "It wasn't the same; it sort of continued from the one yesterday, but I still don't really know what it was about——"

"How can you not know? Didn't it have any logic to it?"

"It's lurid and unreal, but it's like reading on in a story, and now it's just a crazy fragment that I can't even explain." She pulled the sheet up taut and smoothed the blanket. "Turn out the light," she whispered. "I'm okay."

There was a stirring from the other room and Martin hastily hid them in the darkness.

"I called Nicholas and George this morning," Mr. Spiro said. "You are with us so seldom that your brothers should be eager to come in to see you."

Martin bit his lip. That one was double-bladed. He fought back a response.

"But they don't have to come in to see us," Julia said. "It was one of the reasons we didn't bring the kids this time. It would be so much easier for us to go out to see them instead of asking them in for us. . . ."

Her father had a habit of summoning people, and the summoned didn't like it. Julia knew that her brothers were different here, sitting stiffly beside their wives and their stiff, clean children. She had managed to take Martin twice to see them. The visits had been with loved, familiar brothers and generous, proud sisters-in-law.

At home, Nicholas was a quiet, gentle man whose wife, Natalie, brought vivacity and color to his life. Summoned, he was mute as furniture, and Natalie, a loud, exaggerated puppet, talking to fill her lungs with air so that she might be saved from drowning.

At home George was witty in a rather caustic way; his attempt to cover the fact of his amazement at being loved wildly, passionately, and totally by a jolly, maternal wife and five spirited children. Summoned, he became venomous toward everyone, wife and children included, and Grace countered by subsiding into a cowlike acquiescence that heightened the sense of his cruelty while seeming to make it deserved. The family meetings made different people of them all.

Without speaking of it to each other, Julia and Martin each wondered what it made of them. Martin saw himself as being reduced to endless explanation, defense, and apology. He saw Julia, whom he loved and trusted, becoming subtly disloyal and taking her parents' side against him. Julia thought of herself as harried and besieged, at the mercy of one faction and then another. She was shocked that Martin, strong and patient at home, was capricious and unstable here.

"What sacrifice do I ask?" Mr. Spiro demanded. "Not to cut their throats—just to come and see their parents and their sister."

Martin made a last try. "I've been looking forward to visiting separately with Nick and Natalie, and then with George and Grace. I don't know them really well enough, and there's more time to get to talk with each one that way. . . ."

Julia, out of the corner of her eye, caught her mother's shock.

Martin had been talking about getting to know his in-laws, but Mrs. Spiro was hearing only that he wanted to get away from their house, their table—to go anywhere, nowhere, even to the dubious hospitality of Natalie and Grace. Julia had to interrupt him and delicately undercut his point. "Well, we can see them here, of course, and if they do come, we'd be sure of getting together." She knew, guiltily, that Nick and George were always "on call." A visit now would mean that they might not have to come in so soon again and that she and Martin would be here to take on some of the weight of the duty. So much of the daily part of it had been left to Nick and George. . . .

"All right, all right, fine, fine," Martin said. He was helpless and resigned. Julia saw that, too, and wished she could tell him why now. She would explain later. Later he would see all the good reasons.

They dined on the children. "I cook all the delicious Greek food your babies like," the grandmother complained, "but it is too hard and long to bring them to eat it. You once told me you wanted them to know of their heritage from Greece, yet it is too hard to bring them."

"Don't you remember how upset you both were when they came with us last time?" Julia tried to say it without bitterness. "Of course they loved the food, and they think the sun rises and sets on their grandpa and you, but you were upset by their—manners. . . . I just thought we'd all be more relaxed with them at home—until they grow up a bit."

"Julia, if you can't stand a word of criticism, how will you ever learn?"

"It isn't that you criticized them to me; it's what you criticized about. . . ."

She was lost in something she couldn't explain to them, or even to herself. If the boys had misbehaved, whined, broken things or been mulish, she would have been glad of the honesty of the grandparents' irritation. The faults they found, however, were not in what the boys did, but in what they felt, and in what they thought—in a sense, in what they were. ("Why does Timothy seem to have no loyalty? He never defends his little brother. . . . The children have no respect. They speak of their teachers with scorn—of you as if you were their servants. . . . Why does Mark have no sense of the fitness of things? There is nothing on which he will give way.")

These faults were so basic as to be incurable, qualities which were woven into the family plaid of opposing personalities and cross-running needs. There was no way she could tell her parent-judges the differences betwen criticisms of faults of behavior and of faults of being, and that to faults of being they should be allowed no voice. She only sat still.

"Nonsense," Mrs. Spiro was saying. "They are fine little boys, but they are disloyal to the family; that I told you. They must be taught respect."

Martin wondered if eating Greek food would teach them respect. Julia smiled a bit bitterly at her picture of the boys throwing carefully stuffed grape leaves at each other. She sighed and Martin instinctively covered her lapse. "This Greek cheese is wonderful. What do you call it?"

A large, barnlike building. They were lined up before it and went into it one by one. One by one they were stripped and one by one stood shocked in nakedness before the huge light. Her turn . . . The light . . . She staggered backward and heard a quiet voice from beyond the light: "No, no, don't be frightened. You don't want to spoil your beautiful skin by being frightened, do you? See, it is all blotched now. You must never be afraid. You are being made ready for a great fulfillment."

The light was turned off, and when she could see to the sides of the sun-printed after-image in her eyes, there was a small, scholarly man in a doctor's white coat leaning toward her in a kindly way. His manner was calming, almost loving, and after a while she was able to come down from the platform to him when he gestured to her: "Come, I want to show you, to con-

vince you by concern, not by violence, that what I plan to bring to all of you is a benefit, a beauty—the greatest beauty mankind has ever known." He turned and spoke to a guard, "Please bring the demonstration lady in."

Someone else came to the platform naked. The light. The Demonstration Lady moaned in it. "That woman —is—is tattooed!" Julia said, recoiling because the horrible painting covered every inch of the woman's body except her eyes and mouth—great garish swirls of color forming strange swirls like excrescences modeled on her body.

The doctor chided gently, "Of course not. Tattooing is a vulgar, ugly way to achieve the adornment of man's beautiful body. Man wasn't meant to wear clothes, to hide himself, to keep secrets. He was meant to be close to truth, to adorn his body without hiding it guiltily in smelly clothes. Here, on my Island, each one is adorned with mementos of the things he values. This lady, for example, is one of the annual baking-contest winners. We have given her a lovely bread-twist design."

The Demonstration Lady was led away and when the guard took her arm, she screamed.

"Did you see how wonderfully vivid the colors were?" the doctor asked enthusiastically. "How can a tattoo match work done on living flesh?"

"What?"

He said quietly, as if it were self-evident, "We must first remove the skin."

She lay screaming and trembling until the light went on and Martin gave her his presence and the reality of the room. She could only look through the broken edges of her nightmare to where Martin stood with his futile comfort. Then there were the parents to calm again. Their granite manners had fallen away from them in sleep. They were not the dignified, monumental judges of daytime, whose classic strength Martin still half admired, but simply two old people, confused and a little frightened, standing in their nightclothes at the guestroom door like tourists on the brink of a volcano.

Julia looked at them as they were, softened a little by their sleep, and a wave of her childhood's love carried her up in its swift, unreasoning course toward them. She apologized, weeping. It was only a nightmare—too much to eat—because the food had been so delicious. Finally the old people nodded and went back to gather up the fragments of their own night.

Martin sat by her for a while and smoked a cigarette. "Honey, what do you dream about?"

"Not now," she said, and shivered, "not now."

"Julia, this is the third night, and you are obviously dreaming about something horrible. What kind of a dream is it? Is it the same one as before?"

"I had a dream, and then another that sort of followed from it, and this one followed from the second. I'm not trying to hide anything from you; it's just that the dreams are so . . . stupid. It's a nightmare out of a horror comic, a tenth-rate mystery show. It's even got a mad scientist in it. I'd feel silly telling it to you, and I don't even know what it's about." He was going to object, but she looked at him and her eyes were wide with disbelief. "Marty, when I'm dreaming—it's all so real and awful."

"Am I the mad scientist?" he asked, only half kidding.

She shook her head.

He got up and tucked her in like a child, kissing her on the cheek. She smiled and he found himself moved by the smile. Back home there was closeness between them. It was there despite their fights and separate wishes, his job, their house, the kids, the world; but here, with her parents and relatives, he felt vulnerable because he couldn't count on any support from her when he needed it. The smile had reminded him of a real Julia, the one he had left at home. "Don't leave me alone," he said. "Don't leave me here all alone."

"I'll tell you about it when I can. As soon as I can."

He wanted to say he had meant she mustn't leave him alone with the people here.

"Good night, try to sleep. . . ." She was already sleeping.

Sunday breakfast, a ritual. The air was full of hierarchal bells. Romans, Orthodox, and Protestants were all loudly and discordantly summoning the city to its separate togetherness. Mrs. Spiro was rather pointedly missing church for the sake of her transcendent duty to family. Mr. Spiro, who was not a churchgoer, was exulting in his leisure.

"Let me say," he began, pontificating with his knife in the spirit of the bells, "you gave us quite a night. In the Old World dreams were omens. If one had a dream, especially a nightmare, all the old women in the village would be ready to forecast an event. When I came to this country as a boy, my teacher told me that the only thing dreams reflect is too much supper. But since then, I have been reading *The Reader's Digest,* and I see many articles that say how dreams have a meaning."

He looked sharply at Julia. "Have you done something of which you are ashamed?"

"I don't know," she answered and watched his expression cloud with irritation.

"Why is it that you young people can never admit simply what you've done? The bad people say they are sick and the good people say they are really no better than the bad. Either you have obeyed the laws or not; either you have obeyed the moral laws or not."

Julia opened her mouth to speak but thought better of it. Mrs. Spiro had come in with some more hot rolls. "Children, Aunt Thalia called this morning and she wants you to come over to see her. The cousins will be in after church."

Julia and Martin murmured softly about duty rightly done, and ran for their clothes. It would be good to get out, but it would have been unwise to admit loving the scatterbrained, charming old lady and wanting to see her. In the family, duty always seemed to Julia like kissing the whip. If to see someone was a pleasure, it was no duty. If it was no duty, it had no value. In their room they smiled like conspirators.

Aunt Thalia's uncritical lunacy was like the joy of water to tired runners. She could talk and she could listen. She told her own stories and roared with laughter over Julia's which, at a year's remove, had become their family joke.

One day last year the pipes had frozen and burst, Tim was stunned by a falling tree branch, and an animal of some sort had gotten into the house and died somewhere in the heating system. Her calls to the plumber, doctor, and heating man had kept the line busy so that Martin couldn't get through to ask her to bring down a set of case records he had left at home. When he finally got her, too late, he mentioned acidly that she might spend less time gossiping over the phone. This short comment had been greeted with an explosion of bitterness, a recital of his faults, and a flood of tears. Now, the memory was changed. All the facts were the same, only the reality had been altered. It was a joke now, a recital of plagues only the multiplication of which had brought her down. At home, where she was competent, the joke said, such things happened singly all the time, and she foresaw them, fought them, endured them, and cleaned up after them with confident good humor.

Now, as Julia wavered between calling another aunt to prevent jealousy, and checking with her brothers to see if they were coming, she seemed scarcely to believe that the usually level-headed, harassed woman in the story was herself.

Their wonderful Aunt Thalia. . . . When her own children came on *their* summons, she was every bit as demanding and overpowering as Julia's mother, except that her way was petulance and not cold questions. After a few shocked minutes of listening to the eternal complaint—"Where were you last week? Why didn't you call or come to see me? You know I am not well" —Martin began to signal Julia with his eyes. When they were out on the street, he said, "It's bad enough we have to get it in your house—I sure didn't need to hear anybody else getting it."

"That's a terrible thing to say," Julia answered. There was a petulant quality in her voice, perhaps an echo of what they had just been hearing, and it made Martin cringe. She was leaving him alone again.

He sighed, trying to remember that he had to submit only until Thursday. Then they could go home for another year and be happy and sad and a family together in their wretched mistake of a house with old irritations and responsibilities. They seemed very far away and very precious to him.

"Look, honey," he said in a cajoling voice which was irritating even to himself, "why don't we go out together somewhere, just in the afternoons—to a museum, a hospital, a show? Every time we come for a visit we are *there*—there every minute—or else visiting a relative. Let's be mad, reckless, gay. Let's go down to the bank and watch 'em foreclose on a widow. Let's go fish off the pier, Let's———"

She sighed. "It's not worth the trouble. We'd have to go without telling them, or they'd be hurt. Aunt Thalia's calling them now, I bet, or they're calling her. Last time it was because of the kids and this time because of my nightmares. Mother thinks I don't look well. If we go, we'll only have to lie and be questioned. I'm tired; I really haven't had a peaceful sleep since we got here. You go, Marty, I just don't have the energy."

When they got back, Mr. and Mrs. Spiro were in the living room planning the family afternoon with logistics worthy of the Normandy Invasion. They called Julia and Martin in to help with choices which they did not state.

"Let Natalie sit in the middle, between Nick and George," Mr. Spiro said. "I don't care to hear any more about that family tree of hers, or her grandfather or her great grandfather. Put her in the middle."

"A woman should be proud of her husband's family," Mrs. Spiro said, and pursed her lips. Martin tried to keep his expression blank. Every time he or Julia mentioned *his* parents, the woman acted as if he had gotten himself parents for the purpose of irritating her.

"She is always talking nonsense, that one," Mr. Spiro said. "I don't know how Nicholas can put up with it."

"A featherbrain is better than a cow," Mrs. Spiro said. "When George speaks to his wife, he is speaking to a cow. She sits in her fat and smiles like an imbecile."

So much for the in-laws' wives. As if they had forgotten the presence of Julia and the in-law husband, outlaw usurper of her time and duty. Mr. Spiro took a breath and opened his mouth to speak, then perhaps remembered that the flawed creature who had taken his daughter into foreign bondage was present, and he stopped and exhaled. To Martin their recital of complaints seemed to have been habitual, almost formal. He tried to feel that their scorn was general and so should not affect him. In this he failed. He had admired the straight lean strength of Julia's father and the dignity and pride of her mother for so long that their scorn still hurt him. They seemed to have no understanding of why or how he was being given pain if he did not, in fact, deserve it.

"Don't let it happen to your boys, what has happened to Nicholas' children. If Nicholas does not stop that wife of his from ruining them, they will end on the gallows. She's a tramp. She brags about her fine family, but—yes, Julia, she is a tramp!"

Julia had turned away, murmuring "Please" against the relentlessly judging faces before her. Now, Mr. Spiro took up the burden: "You were at college, Julia, a young woman, and nobody wished to tell you such things. He met her in a saloon. She slept with him like a whore for months before they were married. His mother had to wash his underclothes that had her— her body on them."

"At least the Cow waited for a wedding ring——"

"*Mother,*" Julia shouted, desperately and too loud, "Aunt Thalia looked very well today, and we saw Stavros and Maria. Margharita came later, too."

"Yes," Mrs. Spiro countered as a move back to the ground of her target, "Stavros is doing very well."

Martin leapt eagerly behind the change of subject: "I've often wanted to talk to Stavros. Neurology is close to my field, and with new work being done every day in——"

The parents were looking at him in surprise.

"He is a doctor," Mr. Spiro said.

"A Specialist," Mrs. Spiro completed.

They stood together in the bedroom and Julia wrung her hands and kneaded them into one another. "I didn't want to hear things like that about Nick and Natalie— I don't want their secrets—to think about them in a way that's—not my business." Martin wondered why she hadn't chosen to defend *him* against the obvious slur about his being too insignificant to speak to Stavros Who Was A Doctor, A Specialist. But he was too tired to bring it up and it would have been useless anyway. . . .

They tried an extra pillow under Julia's head, hoping it would help, but she was afraid to sleep. She stayed awake for hours, tossing on her bed and staring into the darkness.

The prisoners were silent, but they moaned softly when the wind blew. One could trace the tides of the wind as it came across their raw bodies. They cringed from the heat of the sun, from rain, water, wind. Beds were agony, the rubbing of a sheet, torture. They learned not to touch one another. They were naked. Even if the doctor hadn't been so convinced of the body's decorated beauty, no one was brave enough to endure the touch of clothing. Pain without ease and the feeling of having been distorted and made victims loosened the prisoners' tenuous holds on all the civilizing emotions. No one prayed; no one tried forgetting with art or music, teaching or learning. They drifted out of the sun, the rain, away from sitting or lying down, away from one another, away from themselves. The only happiness that some of the prisoners had was the happiness that they had not brought their children and so were free of their agonies. After the age of nine the children too were "scraped" and decorated with dots or stripes or garish flowers, but sometimes the doctor left them undecorated so that their

veins, pulsing and branched and visible in the raw
flesh made patterns of their own.

Martin came one afternoon to where she was standing out of the sun. She remembered having loved him,
having built a family with him, but now she was
annoyed because he would break into the daydream
she was having.

"I can't take this any more," he said.

She didn't answer.

"I know the general direction of the Landing. There
are three of us—we're going as a team. One is eleven,
one is thirteen, one is grown."

She was still in her daydream, scarcely listening to
him. "Part of us will be killed, but if one gets through,
he will be able to tell——" He spoke without moving his
face or lips, in a dead voice, the habit on the Island,
to save the muscles of the stripped face.

"Good-bye," she said. She was relieved that he had
not asked her to go. She had no more strength for
pain. She went back to the daydream.

"Julia!"

Again. . . . She sat up in bed. "Did I scream?"

"You were moaning. My God, what's happening? I
want to help you, to share it at least, and I can't——"

"Nobody can help me," she said. "Nobody helps
anybody else, and after a while, they stop wanting to."

She sounded resigned and a little self-pitying, and
while he knew that she was talking about the dream,
he couldn't help his own bitterness.

"You're the one who stops helping," he said. "Your
father involves us in things we don't want, and when I
need you to stand against them, you fade away on me
and I'm left as the big Destroyer, the Outlander Who
Doesn't Know What Family Means."

"They come with so many *reasons,*" she said. "I can't fight them with nothing."

"Your reasons should be that I don't *want* them. One—I don't want a family party. Two—I don't want to sit and smile and let them pick me apart. Three—I don't want to spend every single day of my vacation doing these things. . . . I just don't want to and when I say so, Julia, I want you to defend me."

"But I *can't.* Don't you see? I know why they are criticizing you, and that it doesn't even involve you personally. They may love us, Marty, but they're afraid."

They were sitting up in bed. It was still dark, but only gray-dark. They had this hour or two of private time before the day began . . . and the party. Ordinarily, they might have made love, but they both found it hard to do with Julia's parents sleeping in the next room. There was also the change in each of them that made them strange to each other.

She tried to tell him about the summoning and the denials. A Greek family, she said, is supposed to be *one.* The parents had both grown up with that, and for many years, poverty and strangeness had made it so. They huddled together in close family business, made "good" marriages for the family, formed no friendships that might rival the unity they needed to survive. This was the dream, the picture, the hope— a huge family, all together, all one.

"The ideal would be a kind of family world. You're sick—you go to Stavros; you're in trouble—you call Nicholas, the lawyer. You want clothes—George has a store. America is a big place; it's got too many choices. A world is frightening if it is bigger than a small Greek village. But see what happened—Stavros decided to specialize in something nobody ever got sick from; Nicholas moved away *because* he didn't want to be a lawyer, but an engineer. Who needs engineers in a small

Greek village? When George found that getting his own business meant that everyone depended on deliveries, free, any time, any place, he moved out too. They raised us to fit in the picture, but we didn't want it and we destroyed it."

". . . And you married a speech therapist who works with aphasics and wants to live in a small town."

All right, he thought. Now they both knew the reasons for the picking and poking and criticism, but understanding had taken the fight out of Julia and would probably blunt his own will to resist. The very choice that frightened the parents had given strength to the children. The family parties then, were partly funerals, with little cakes and speeches about the virtues of the dead. Unfortunately, the dead were very much alive, living in the enemy world—thriving in it. Angry funerals. The present children had murdered the children who were supposed to be there, close, self-nourishing, ideal.

He saw why Julia couldn't defend him—she was fighting shadows. He leaned back and looked at her. He could make out her features now. It was almost day; the night of bad dreams was being pried up from the rim of the world. It was quiet; they were alone, stealing peace. But the day they were facing was one he dreaded. His wife had horrible dreams from which she woke screaming; her family had dreams from which they could not wake at all; and he, too, felt his will dissolving as the days passed. Yet he had nothing with which to engage. He sighed and turned to her. "It looks like a nice day. Why don't we go for a walk?"

"I wish I could," she said listlessly, "but Mother will be cooking and baking for the big get-together this afternoon and she hates to do that alone. You know what the pattern is—the women for their men . . ."

"The pattern, the pattern . . . I know."

The relatives came to the house almost on tiptoe. They greeted Julia and Martin as though something not to be admitted had kept them away for so long. Julia was puzzled by the almost sacerdotal stillness until she realized that it must be because of the dreams— four nights of screaming, whimpering, and moaning, cut off by commands of the indecent, secret-keeping husband. It must have been made public knowledge: one with Natalie's manias and morals, and Grace's bovine calm. Everyone knew, but not in the comfortable Greek way of omens of the imponderable future. Her parents were not the only students of Reader's Digest which spoke of present guilt and past shame and Julia, in her misery, hoped that Martin didn't understand the reason for the soft voices and the clumsy, well-meant concern. She had never, until this day, considered herself possessed by the dreams instead of being their possessor. Now, with the fact of her nightmares the property of everyone, she began to wonder at her mind's power to conceive of them. Night after night, she had gone back to circle over that man and woman as they walked stripped bare, all the defining, protecting skin peeled away, suffering agony for the whim of a madman. Yet suddenly, in the middle of her relatives' muted gentling, she had come to see the horror of it, and herself not as Julia, but as Someone Who Dreamed, whose dreams hung over her in shock like the sky after lightning.

Their compassion frightened her, and the more she felt them soothing and agreeing, the more frightened she was. From across the room Martin looked at her in puzzlement, and when he could break away, he came over and whispered, "What is it, honey? You look all flushed."

"It's nothing."

"What's it all about? Everybody is acting as if

there'd been a death in the family and they're trying hard not to mention it."

A death! She shuddered.

"Honey"—he took her arm gently as if to try to convince her of something (Aunt Thalia looked and then looked away. Stavros looked and then looked away.)—"Why don't you sneak out and lie down and rest awhile?"

For a minute she thought of telling him that her parents had chosen to be disloyal to both of them. Brothers and sisters-in-law who hadn't seen her for a year and knew nothing about her life, knew now that she had nightmares and that she screamed her way free of them. She began to tell him, but before two words were out, she had to stop. He was too vulnerable. He would be furious and thwarted. What was there to do or say that wasn't more madness and more bad dreams?

"I can't go," she said. "They'd miss me and this afternoon is supposed to be for us, after all. I'll be all right." She smiled up at him and he let himself be silenced because of the people all around him. He dipped back into his well of duty. Grace, Aunt Tecla, and Aunt Thalia were arguing happily until he came and struck silence. For the tenth time that afternoon, he began, in a mystified way, to weave a conversation with thin air.

Now that Julia knew what had happened, she was free to look around and see how the afternoon was going. They were all acting, talking themselves past her haunted house, and it did them good actually, until her parents spoke to them. Natalie had been a little muted, George was less vitriolic, Stavros and Aunt Thalia acted with good nature, the roles written for them, but whenever The Parents joined a group in conversation, a kind of helpless anguish bloomed in their presence.

At last it was time to serve. There were huge plates of Greek food and glasses of raisin wine and ouzo, for which no one had much appetite, since the meal came between lunch and dinner. The guests seemed almost unwilling to sit close to one another.

There were toasts: To the ones who live so far—may they find with their own people the peace of mind they have lost.

Whose own people? Martin's family hadn't even been invited.

At last everyone had eaten all he could be urged to eat and had begun to signal and mouth words: ". . . the baby sitter. . . . We promised around six . . ." and raise the voice a little for finality: "It certainly was a wonderful afternoon, really."

By six-thirty they had all gone. When the door closed on Aunt Tecla, Martin went limp with the release and Julia's eyes fell into the fixed, glazed look that they had been fighting all day. She was exhausted.

Mr. Spiro was just getting his second wind: "I don't like George's eyes—they were almost yellow. He smokes too much."

His wife nodded him on. "Did you notice? His fingers trembled. He works too hard supporting that fat cow and all those children."

Her husband made no comment, but went on with his own thought: "Nicholas is getting fat. A man should not lose to a woman—to be made like a pet dog."

"Did you notice Stavros?" Mrs. Spiro asked. "His eyes are pure, like a saint. Did you see how he always waited for the Mother to speak?" She sighed.

"Stavros will wait to marry."

"Stavros will not marry a streetwalker."

"If only the children had come. I think they are trying to keep the children from us."

"Children are not raised well any more."

"Julia didn't even bring her children—why should the others?"

Julia was thinking that they hadn't brought the children because one does not bring children to a place where someone is insane.

One-Is-Eleven, One-Is-Thirteen, One-Is-Grown. They crept into the path of sunrise's blinding light, murmuring in pain. They eased into the water, biting pain into the small sticks they kept in their mouths for it. When they were far enough away from the Island, they struck out toward the west, swimming through foul water and fresh, watching snakes thread the water and the slow eyes of swamp creatures following them.

The effort of bending and stretching was great, but they were away, free. They would have to get to the Landing by nightfall. Stroke, bite down, rest, stroke. One-Is-Eleven tried to swim faster because he was the youngest and was guilty about holding them back. He swam faster and faster and hit the electrified grid before he knew it. The water boiled up and then was still. The two others swam dumbly through the grid which had been shorted out by One-Is-Eleven's body. They went on, winding through mazes of sawgrass and pools through which fish swam. The sun was almost at noon now. Stroke, bite, rest, stroke. They became afraid of swimming endlessly in circles dying by minutes until night, and death by snake or quicksand.

One-Is-Thirteen was beginning to lag. He was exhausted. He saw the alligator settle in the water and glide toward One-Is-Grown. He began to think wildly of all the moments of power and love a grown man could have, but not being grown himself, he missed the quality of those moments and their weight. He thought of the love that bonded families together. Then One-Is-Thirteen saw the man forcing the crocodile's jaw shut. He thought at that moment of the uncertain quality of family love—too much, too little, love given or denied at the wrong time. The alligator clawed the man's raw flesh. One-Is-Thirteen thought desperately of a spring day when he had gone for a walk with his mother, stopping to look at each miracle of the new season. The man had his hold on the alligator's mouth and was holding the creature under water to drown it. Then, without being able to stop, One-Is-Thirteen began to see his mother in ambiguous scenes—playing cards, gossiping, irritated at his interruptions, blaming him unfairly. The alligator gave a great roll in the water, freed itself, and turned on One-Is-Grown, breaking his neck and shoulder in its awful jaws. One-Is-Thirteen swam on. He was dimmed with pain and weakness; he noticed nothing, he had no hope or plan. Stroke, bite, rest, stroke. The sun rode low. It began to go behind the great overhung trees. Nocturnal things began to wake and prepare themselves for their hunger. Ahead of him the swamp stopped. It was the Landing. . . .

The naked, red boy appeared like a horrid ghost. They people of the Landing saw him and couldn't believe what they saw. A man came over to where One-Is-Thirteen stood at the very edge of the water, looked at him and went back, nodding in amazement.

"He has no skin." Then the man went up to the boy again, and back. "Look how he is." Again the man came back. "What happened, boy? Tell us what happened."

One-Is-Thirteen opened his mouth to tell them how the sun seethed on the prisoners' bodies and cracked their flesh, about the mild madman and the beautification colors, the electric grid, the alligator, the ones who died, the way the Island moaned when the wind came up, the Decorated Ones. He stood there with his mouth opened, thinking of the Island, wanting to speak, to

tell them. The men of the Landing waited and en-
couraged him. "Come on, son, we're not going to hurt
you." But he could not speak. He tried again and
again. No sound. Night fell. One by one the people of
the Landing turned and went to their houses and the
mute boy stood alone and beginning to die, in the
empty street.

This time Julia was crying when Martin woke her.
She found herself awake in the middle of a wail of
sorrow. She cut off the second and looked up at him
and then at the door. No one was there, but she knew
that the parents were awake, listening in the blind
night. "Are you all right?" he whispered.

"Yes. . . ." and she slept again.

At breakfast they were all silent. What evil they
must think she had done to be so tormented! Martin
wanted her to tell him what the dreams were, but she
didn't truly know. In the end they seemed not fearful
so much as despairing. One-Is-Thirteen (she had no
trouble seeing the three of them as one man at different
ages), having come all that way, knowing the horror in
his own flesh, could say nothing, and in the end, could
do nothing. She kept seeing him as she had left him,
a small, lone figure in the small street, dying.

Today was the day Julia had been given to call her
old friends, but she didn't call anyone. She was too
tired. The dream, now completed, hung between herself
and the world, dimming it and blurring her picture of
herself in it—the competent, aware person she was at
home. Tonight they would begin to pack and tomorrow they would leave. But it wouldn't be the same,
even at home. She felt like an invalid being sent away
for "rest," and it was nearly true—having been spoken
to gently in a dozen phone calls during the morning.

After breakfast she washed some clothes slowly, trying to pull out the time. Then she did her hair and set it . . . slowly . . . slowly. And the clock said 10:05. The day was rising like a tidal wave, vast and impersonal. Her mother talked; her father talked. She answered them automatically, promising everything, agreeing to anything. After a while Martin came in and she answered him automatically, promising and agreeing. "It's your day out, Julia."

"I'm so tired—"

"For godsake! We can't stay cooped up here all day. I've got to get out!"

"Well, why don't you go?" She thought: Why doesn't he go and leave me in peace? Then she stopped, caught something in the past somewhere. Did he say that before? Someone had said that before and she had thought it—no, someone else . . . "Where is there to go?"

"Burma, Mozambique, the park. Come on, will you? Tie something on those martian rollers and let's break out. The guards have been drugged, the watchdogs tied—or is it the other way around? Put on your lipstick and we're over the wall. *Come on!*" he said. Even in his quips there was a desperation that was disturbing. "Please before they sound the alarm."

The picture of the electric grid came to her mind. The guard had pressed a place in a tree. It slid up, dripping water. It had been waiting in the water for One-Is-Eleven. Then there was his body tangled in it.

"Julia, please—come on!"

It was too bright outside; the glare burned her eyes. "I want to go home," she said.

"I know. We'll be home tomorrow night, and it'll be all right after that." He had thought she meant their home and not her parents'. She let him think it.

"Some vacation," he went on. "You *dream* and I

end up feeling like a cuticle bitten down to the quick. It happens every time. It beats me, this whole business. I get so torn up, I'm nothing but a raw, quivering ego. And next time we'll have to bring the kids."

She walked another block in silence and then stopped suddenly, almost accusingly in the middle of the sidewalk. "What did you say?"

"I said we'd have to bring—"

"Before that."

"I didn't mean it maliciously, and I didn't say it to get a rise out of you. It's true. I said I felt like a quivering . . . raw ego."

She looked at him for a minute and then she began to laugh. He stood by helplessly, wishing he could forget himself in laughter too, while people passed them half ashamed to smile in case she was laughing at him. "Back there you said it was a prison." She began to walk again. "You said, 'Let's break out.' "

"Forget it. I don't want to get into another——"

"No, it was good. You rescued me, in a way. I've been having these dreams, and what you said was what I was dreaming about."

"I don't get it."

"I got it. Technicolor and Panavision, and it's something close to what you said about being a raw ego. I haven't figured it all out yet, but let me tell you what I know. In the beginning, there were letters. To the Members of the D.A.R. and other groups. It gathered them at a small Greek village, exotic to me, and isolated. In the village there was a patriarch and he decided what the villagers should become. But the villagers weren't born there—they came from many places and they came to the village in love. Natalie came, so proud of her illustrious family, and Grace, so proud of her homemaking. Imagine, a baking-contest lady. And you and I came together, in love. The patriarch. . . . He wishes he could love us too, but we

seem always to be hiding. He strips us of our secrets
and weakens us with their loss so we cannot escape.
But you escape, Martin; you escape."

She was shivering in the summer heat. He stepped
away from her for a moment because he was frightened by her. She looked as she had when she had broken
the night screaming after one of those dreams. Then he
moved back, close, to try to comfort her. "Julia——"

"I was so weakened that I betrayed you. You had
to go alone—more than alone. Oh, God, you had to
go *divided*."

She looked almost as if she were arguing and people
walked around them with a quickened pace so as not
to be involved. "Then"—and she half-smiled as more
of the pieces fit—"two thirds gone, and the best two
thirds you thought, you got to safety, to freedom, to a
'landing,' and what was there to say then?"

"Come on, honey, let's go to the park. Okay? And
pick out a bench and sit there and talk like old, old
people. You're scared, or maybe angry, and I——"

"Not scared any more," she said. "Ashamed. I'm so
sorry and so ashamed. Seven years of it, and how I
betrayed you. No wonder I felt so lost in the boat—
coming to my own deception."

"But you said the dream had a mad scientist——"

"He's not our problem; I am. The problem is deception. If there's any defense, it is that my secrets and
our lives were taken from me against my will. I never
meant. . . . I don't know to this minute how I can
change things—or if I can change them—but for this
minute, right now, I know what I've done to you, and
I'm ashamed, and I want to try to *do* something——"

"We're going home early tomorrow. It will be all
right."

"No!" she shouted. "It will definitely not be all
right. I want to remember the whole, ugly, awful thing.
It was why it was so ugly, I guess. You were electro-

cuted and eaten by a crocodile. In the end, you weren't even able to tell anyone about what had happened."

"Good Lord, girl, I have days like that all the time!"

"But then you come home and I'm there."

"And then *we* eat the crocodile."

"If you'd finished yours yesterday, you wouldn't have to put up with the leftovers."

"I can hardly wait," he said.

9   Timekeeper

ROY KNEW HE WAS an impatient man; people told
him so often enough. Marty, his partner, used to make
bad jokes about it; but the way Roy experienced this
weakness in himself was not as the perpetrator of rude-
ness or bad manners, but as a victim. Roy waited. He
waited in line at stores, banks, and post offices. He
waited, changing his packages from hand to hand, ticking with his tongue, his heels rising and falling like
muted hammers that strike the hour: It is time, it is
time. His fingers would drum: his jaw would work in
a grinding rhythm: he would feel the beat of blood
in his head and a swelling rage at it all, while the un-
caring clerks at the windows counted change, counted
change, counted change. He waited for his wife to go
or to come or to dress or to undress, and at last he
waited in the hospital corridor, drumming his fingers
and tapping his foot, desperately for the drugs to work
and then the surgery. But her pulse lost time and the
beat of her heart stilled. He waited for buyers and
salesmen who came late and repairmen who sometimes
didn't come at all.

Now he was waiting in the doctor's office, promised again and again deceived. They had told him his appointment was at three. It's a *contract,* he insisted to himself, a promise; I was here at three! And he sighed, his fingers beginning to drum on the table. The woman across from him glared, and he transferred the drumming to his knee. The waiting room was discouragingly full. He glanced at each of the other patients surreptitiously, measuring them as they sat with blank faces, their suffering hidden decently by their clothes. Fifteen minutes. He picked over the pile of magazines, selected one, and began to turn the pages. When he was waiting, he found he could never commit himself deeply to anything else. The fact of his waiting wouldn't let him go.

Thirty-five minutes now. A contract, and they had broken it, and he was being kept against his will, waiting, committed by the time he had already spent, like a bad business deal. He began to riffle quickly through another magazine. The other side of the waiting room stared at him impassively. Marty was always kidding him about his impatience. "You live like a bomb—ticking off minutes for an explosion." Maybe so, but still, he had been successful, and he was still, still alive.

Which Marty was not, for all his ease and kidding. Roy's eye broke out of focus on the magazine page, and the picture of the watch there went double. This past year had been hell to live through alone. They had been in business together for fifty-four years, he and Marty. They had started with two rolls of reeking brocade, a giveaway from Sobelski's after the fire. Two sixteen-year-old boys and two rolls of water-hosed brocade.

When he tried, he could remember all the gears and wheels, springs and coils of circumstances and events that fitted into the stores and his life and Marty's. He could remember how many false starts, mistakes, and complications there had been between that brocade and getting the first store, then enlarging it and getting the second and the third. What he couldn't remember was when Marty's face had begun to sag with age, when his eyelids had thickened and the jowls came. He had never stopped thinking of himself and Marty as kids together, even after both of them were married, Marty a grandfather and himself a widower. Sometimes they had even said it: "Hey, kid, what can we do with the shipment of muslin?" He never meant it ironically. If a stock boy snickered, he thought it was because of the difference in address—that Marty wasn't really "Mr. Dowben," but "kid."

Then, the year before last, one day in the middle of summer, when the woolens were just beginning to come in for fall and there was planning to be done and a new sales campaign, an old man had come up to him—a man with a wrinkled, jowled face and veined hands. And it was Marty. Roy had been so shocked that he stood and stared and then looked away, to try to hide the shock, and he could barely hear what Marty was saying to him.

They went to lunch, the old man still calling him "kid," although Roy could no longer say it.

At lunch, Marty began to tell him what had happened. "You know, I haven't been feeling too good lately. I went to the doctor yesterday, and he told me I couldn't stay with the business full time if I wanted to see seventy. I told him I couldn't leave the business —what should I do? I asked if couldn't stay at least until after Christmas. He said it was out of the question. I said October, then—at least for the fall sale. He said I'd have to work half time or he wouldn't be responsible."

The face looked so stunned and puzzled by its own heaviness and age that Roy had to struggle to get his mouth smiling and his shoulders moving to shrug, as if Marty's worries were nothing.

"You had me scared for a minute. With three stores and a wife wanting a vacation the first time in forty-five years, why not play hooky for the winter?" He leaned over, trying to sound easy and jovial. "Where does she want to go? The Islands? Hawaii?"

"I hadn't really thought of going anywhere. I wanted to talk to you first. Roy—I don't *want* to retire."

Roy overplayed his casualness a little. There was no question of retiring, only taking a break, resting up, getting a little strength back.

Marty didn't make it through October, even on three hours a day. His hands lost their co-ordination, so that his writing was barely legible, and he began to make silly mistakes with numbers, two hundred and ten when he meant twelve hundred, and countersigning the errors when his secretary caught them and sent them back with cruelly polite question marks penciled in lightly beside them. His vacation plans were never mentioned again. In September, he stopped working but came in anyway, haunting the stores until the stores were haunted by his illness. It was overwhelming him. By December, he was at home, alternately shrill and passive before the television set. By spring, even television's unchanging plots were beyond him.

The last year was the year of the hospital, and a death wrung cell by cell from a brutal salvation-by-force. In a way, his death, finally, was a kind of triumph. Without mind or memory, he had fought the pumping, clicking Existence Machines for a year and had won—a man successful enough, even with taxes and college and house payments, to pay for that year's agony all by himself, without going begging.

Someone in the waiting room coughed, a hard,

hollow cough that brought Roy back from the last pictures he had of Marty. He found himself still staring at the advertisement of the wristwatch, and he looked around guiltily, hoping that no one had noticed his taking all that time, peering like an idiot at a picture of a watch. No one moved, no one breathed, and his eye fell back to the magazine.

It was a nice presentation, that picture; it was well done. When he and Marty had started to expand, they had found that the big ads they were putting in the papers weren't enough, and they got a man in to design something more ambitious. Advertising was a thing for which neither of them had any particular gift; they let the experts handle it. It was hard to tell if the advertising did any good, really, or if it was the Muzak or the new windows; but it was part of the way things ran now, and some of what the advertising men said had stuck with him.

He studied the page again. Very effective. It was an engraving of a wristwatch that seemed to hold the solar system inside the circle of its band. There was just the word "Helichron" at the top and then the picture and nothing else, except way down at the bottom of the page, where it wouldn't distract the eye. He began to read: "A watch running on a tiny, powerful, replaceable solar battery has certain distinct advantages. Ask your jeweler."

He half rose and leaned over so he could see the clock behind the receptionist's desk. Fifty minutes. A fifty-minute wait. What did they think he was? He ran a large business; he had had dealings with buyers and union men and merchandising men and bankers and brokers, and none of them had kept him sitting waiting outside an office for fifty minutes! He was about to get up and leave in disgust when the receptionist called his name and a nurse came and ushered him into one of the offices. She told him in a rote way to take his clothes off and put on the examination gown provided. Before he could say anything, she was gone.

There was nothing to do but go ahead and strip. The examination gown was a little white paper thing, and wearing it seemed somehow to reduce him. He stood humbled in it, his legs sticking out bare and pale, and he felt suddenly like a victim, sicker in some intangible way than by the sickness that had brought him here. They know, he thought, those doctors. The waiting softens you up, and this puts the clincher on it. If you don't advertise, you have to have ways to keep the customers coming back. A little good old fear is all it takes. And he chuckled and tried to feel better.

The doctor came in and apologized briskly and automatically for the long wait. He asked some questions in an impersonal, not unfriendly professional manner, pausing as if to tick off possibilities on a chart that Roy could not see. The physical examination was simple, and much of it was like those he had had when he was a child, with the familiar thumpings and requests that he cough.

When he had dressed again, he was shown into another office, with books and diplomas, and now the doctor's careful professionalism was a little distracting. Roy wondered if he might really be very ill and the doctor was hedging, hiding the bad news.

"You've got a few little things that bear watching," the doctor said. "Nothing exceptional for a man of your age, but I'd like you to come in for some more tests—in the morning, before you've eaten—and we'll need a urine specimen. If you'll see the nurse outside, I've checked off the tests we'll need, and she has the instructions all ready, so you'll know just what to do. In case there's another attack of the dizziness and pain you complained of, I've ordered some of these for you." He handed the usual, eternal, illegible prescription across the desk.

Roy took it, rising heavily and carefully in his newly fragile body. He thanked the doctor, who had turned to something else and looked back at him with a little annoyance. Before he left, Roy made his appointment at the nurse's desk and took the printed sheet of instructions humbly. Then, with a lift of self-righteous pride, he walked, successful, past the chairs of the other petitioners, who still waited.

He came to himself on the street, clutching the instruction sheet and the prescription in his hand. He read the sheet. "Do not take liquids for a twelve-hour period before—" He looked away from the instructions to the street, and he saw Marty, hung with tubes, a vacant being, a ghost, moaning in that pleasant, pleasant room. And now he was letting them begin it with him. Here he was on a fine afternoon, a man who could work a full day, a man with business to transact, with a life that was his now, a man still standing up in his clothes, thank God, and now he was going to let them put paper dresses on him and reduce him to the numbing mumble of machines. "No!" he said quite loudly into the argument, and stepping over to a litter basket, shredded the prescription and the instructions into it and walked away.

Two weeks later, he was going from his office in the main store to have lunch with an importer when the dizziness came again, and the ache, riding spurs into his back. He stopped, waiting for the pain to slow and his eyes to clear. He was sweating; his palms, forehead, waist and groin were suddenly wet with it. He was terrified. As the first blackness passed, warmth came flooding back and a too-rapid, sickish easing that replaced the chill of the sweat. He tried to walk again as if nothing had happened, fighting to remember where he was going and whom he was to meet. He lost his breath again and had to stop by a building until he could get it back. The second grayness and dizziness faded slowly. His mind cleared. He was all right now —it was just a little spell.

When he came to the hotel, he felt a brief return of the pain; but since there was no dizziness with it, he went on into the restaurant and was shown to the table where the importer was already waiting.

The man greeted him, and then his face began to show concern. "Are you all right? You look a little pale."

Roy reassured the importer and himself, ordering a big lunch and sitting back to talk with careful patience. As they ate, he motioned toward the importer's wrist. "That watch you are wearing—is that a special watch? I seem to remember seeing one like it somewhere."

"Yes, it's a Helichron." The importer laughed, indulging himself. "It operates on solar batteries." He moved his shirt sleeve up and took off the watch to show it to Roy. "See—" He turned it over and snapped it open. The usual delicately balanced miniature universe of wheels and gears was absent. Inside the thin metal shell there were only three small gears, two little wire leads, the posts from which they hung and a small milled nickel capsule resting to one side. "They've got these batteries, so they store a year's supply of power. When the year is up, you take them to the watchmaker, he pops in another battery, attaches those leads, and there you are. The batteries hardly cost anything, and there's no winding and no setting. It keeps perfect time."

"Don't you ever set it?" The importer smiled tolerantly, and Roy noticed that there was no winder button on the watch. "But what if it slows down?"

"This works just like an electric clock. You never need to adjust that unless your power quits, and this battery lasts for a year."

"But when it starts to lose power—"

"That's the part I like best. When the battery begins to go, the watch stops automatically. It's one of the qualities of this battery, but they've put some kind of governor in there, too, just to make sure—because you get to depend on a watch like this."

"And the batteries are easy to get?"

"Unless you're going to Peru. They have one of their main stores about three blocks from here, as a matter of fact, up on Van Allen, but any watchmaker can replace the batteries. If you have a steady hand, they'll sell you a little tool and you can replace them yourself." He closed the back of the watch with a delicate scratch-snap that made a pleasing sound. "Gadgets, I love 'em. Most of them don't work, but this watch is really something."

"Well," Roy said slowly, "I guess I don't really *need* a watch. Everywhere you go there's a clock, nowadays. I can't remember when I needed a watch last." For some reason he couldn't explain, he didn't want the man to know how taken he was with the watch, as if that revelation were too deep and personal and would compromise him in some way.

When Roy left the restaurant after lunch, he had a solid feeling of satisfaction. His pain was gone; he had come close to working out the arrangements on a deal for $85,000 worth of Italian and Japanese silk. He didn't want to go back to the office right away. He wanted to walk a little, to make sure that the pain and dizziness were really gone, to prove that his body was his own again. So he walked to the store on Van Allen Street, listened shyly while a clerk demonstrated and explained, and then bought the watch.

He soon found himself as eager as the importer had been to snap off the back of his watch and reveal its simplicity, its worklessness. In the beginning, he could hardly believe that the watch would keep time without any winding and setting. He didn't have to begin any of its rhythms, willing it to go, as he did when he wound a watch—to endure that little moment's death unril the gears engaged and Cause rolled over into Effect. The watch simply went.

Lucius, at the branch store, began to kid him about it, and when the cashiers and bookkeeper saw that he liked the kidding, they joined in: "What time is it, Mr. B.?"

"Look at the clock," he would say gruffly. "The union says we have to have a clock for the clock watchers."

"But that clock doesn't give the latest time. The clock in the Lincoln Street store is five minutes faster."

"Well, Lincoln Street is east of here"—he would clear his throat—"different time zone." And then he would push up his sleeve majestically and give them the time. It was always at variance with the wall clock, and it was always correct. (The bookkeeper checked it by phone time.) The other stores soon picked up the joke, and it settled into the vacuum that had been left by the end of joking about Marty and his bargains and his golf manners. The wound was being healed.

Roy's loneliness, too, was slowly easing. They had a very good back-to-school season this year. Before he could think, they were into the late-fall season. Then there were Christmas, cruise season, a big pre-spring sale and closeout, graduation and bridal, vacation season and on again through the summer closeout and back to school. These commercial seasons superseded the other more natural divisions of the year, but they, too, came in their rhythm and followed one another in faithful order into time past. To Roy they were not a boring round of buying and selling; they had come to be more meaningful to him than the seasons of

present weather, and it comforted him to know that
there were still people going back to school. He would
have been content if it weren't for the spells of dizziness
and pain.

There were days when he couldn't believe he had
ever suffered. Weeks went by when he would lift bolt
after bolt of cloth impatiently out of the stock boy's
hands and run up the ladders to show them how to slide
the heavy rolls into place on the shelves without
bunching or wrinking the fabric. He tore miles of
goods into mountains of remnants, relishing both the
feel of the cloth and the sound of its tearing.

Then there were other weeks, long weeks, when his
body seemed unable to recoup its lost strength, and it
took all his effort and will to make it rise in the morning, dress, and do what he asked of it. At these times,
he forced it to work, hour by hour, through the day.
If those were the terms, so be it.

But the terms were the terms of the enemy, and
they were deceptive. The dizziness might wait a month,
two months, three. The pain might streak back and
forth across the corridors of his nerves to and from its
hiding places and then sink to sleep. It slumbered, hidden, and grew fat in his good fortune. Then, at no
signal he could name, for no reason he could trace,
dizziness and pain would break upon him suddenly
with a relentless pounding at his back and a blackness
before his face. In those sieges, he would promise himself desperately that he was going to see the doctor
again and to submit to all the specialists' Procrustean
beds; but in an hour the black-white faintness would
fade to gray, and the nausea would ease, and in a day
or two the pain would tire itself out, and in a week,
shrunken like a sullen dwarf it would limp away again
to sleep. Then his terror would dissolve into anxiety,
the anxiety into a cautious acceptance, the acceptance

into a humble joy at the ease and beauty there were in a day's work and a night's sleep.

But he knew the time was slowly narrowing between these attacks and that he was tiring himself trying to outrace them. And in his tiredness and fear, he knew he was beginning to make mistakes. He had, among other things, been foolish in overlooking the impact of the pop-art fabric that had taken hold all over the country. He had waved it off as a fad for the teen-agers, those crazy patterns and nightmare colors. How many dresses could anyone stand as loud as that? Once the market was sated, the fad would stop; it would be finished, out, in a way he had seen a hundred times before; an invisible thumb turned down between Tuesday night and Wednesday morning, and thousands of dollars of stock left untouched on the shelves.

A smart goods-man hedges on fads or he loses his shirt. Who would have believed that grown women, middle-aged, grandmothers even, would suddenly begin to cut short shifts out of that heartburn cloth, flesh unto flesh? By the time he saw the mistake, it was already too late. He tried to pass it off to himself, but he knew he hated the vibrating loudness of those new fabrics because they reminded him of his illness and his fear.

In the grip of this fear, he found himself consciously trying to change some of his ways, to be more patient. Impatience ran so deep in him that the work of changing was highly visible. His managers noticed it and were confused and uncomfortable. Keeley, at the Lincoln Street store, began to shift his feet and make excuses whenever Roy conquered the nervous urgency and forced himself to relax and talk about the weather or politics or even sex. Keeley had always been the one to stop him from leaving right away: "Oh, Mr. B.——" and telling a joke to keep him. Roy had been pleased to be kept from leaving, because Keeley did it out of a liking for him. Now they all thought up reasons to get away. It saddened him to think of it—five minutes and they were tearing their hair.

One day he had heard Stillson, in the Halstead Boulevard store, talking about him, and he was embarrassed.

"He can't even let anybody else close the stores," Stillson's assistant had said.

"Oh, he's always been that way, but now it seems so much more important to him."

Tuesday and Thursday nights the main store stayed open until ten. The two branch stores were open on Thursday only, and they closed at nine. After Roy's wife died, he had gotten in the habit of closing one of the branch stores and then going back to Lincoln Street, where his office was, and checking on last-minute things. It took about an hour to finish after closing time. Once the main lights were turned out, the aisles had to be swept and the dust covers put over the counters. Bolts of cloth that had been left out were rolled up and put back on the shelves. The day's receipts were added, the money was put in the safe, and the registers were made up for the next day's opening.

Even before Marty died, Roy had been the one to snap the door shut at the main store, to be the very last one out. Now, even though Keeley had been with him for twenty years, Roy felt an increasing need to do that last thing of the day. If he was seeing one of his few friends or had stopped, during one of the difficult times, to take in a movie, he would leave, in order to get back and close up.

Tonight he had left the Cherrydale West store and decided to stop for a bite to eat in another part of the shopping center. He thought of going back after his dinner and waiting until the store was ready to close, but then decided against it. It wasn't good to visit and then come back the same day. The employees felt you didn't trust them: it was bad for morale. So he had about three and a half hours to kill between now and the time they would be locking up for the night at the other branch. Then, of course, he would go to Lincoln Street.

The weather was nice, and he didn't want to waste time in the movies. For a moment he turned outside the restaurant and paused uncertainly, and then the idea came to him exactly what he wanted to do. Most of the other stores were open tonight too. It had been years since he had nosed around and seen what the competition was up to. He had a sudden feeling of delight; he felt like a movie spy, a secret agent passing himself off as an ordinary shopper.

It was funny, because Marty had always been the one who went to "take a look." Marty loved to go into other stores; in the stupidest hick towns, he would be drawn toward any place where a person could buy a yard of dress goods. Once his car broke down in a spot called Pigeon River, and he came back with one of his stories. "The storekeeper's name was Oetker—what a merchandiser! He had three bolts of goods: a brown wool and a bolt of gray chambray with a little blue stripe. That's the winter and the summer. That was for fashions. Then he had one bolt of stripped canvas —you know, mattress ticking. That was the decorator bolt. Now, what was funny was that this was okay with everybody in Pigeon River. I didn't see anyone who wasn't wearing something in that gray chambray with the little stripe, and if I'd been there in the winter, I swear it would have been brown wool, like uniforms. And from the decorator bolt—"

How they laughed then, when the business was the one store, Marty and Keeley and Eubanks and himself! The partners and two salesmen, and they all did everything. How much they enjoyed the days and all the little things that happened—or was it just in memory, with the doubts resolved and the gambles having worked after all? Back then, somebody would call and ask to speak to the buyer, and they would shout, "Buyer! Buyer to the phone, please!" Then they would laugh to each other, "Buyer and janitor, and that's value for the money!"

Those days were good, but *these* days were good too. You had to stop and think about it, but it was true, even with the union and taxes and the bigness of it all. The merchandise was better now; the salesmen didn't have to try to talk customers out of returning things, as they used to. One mistake wasn't a catastrophe.

He walked through the shopping center to the big department store and went up on the escalator to the yard-goods department. Then, as he stood before the beckoning plenty of it all, he remembered why it had been Marty and not he who had gone around to "case the competition." How strange to have forgotten something so painful and so much a part of him. It was the jealousy. How could he have forgotten how bitterly, wretchedly jealous he would become if the goods in the other store were fine and the place was carpeted? He hadn't been able to stand it, in the end, and had left the visiting to Marty. Now that, too, had changed. He was free of it at last. He smiled; at least you could outgrow some things; there was some mercy waiting.

He was walking easily and happily up and down the spacious, well-lit aisles. He noticed how well they displayed their quality merchandise. They weren't taking advantage of their remnant counters, though, and the out-of-season things were set too far back for the customers to see. They were underselling him in most of their woolens, and they had some textured synthetics he had never seen, but his silk and Dacron were still far ahead and the cottons nicely competitive. Secret agent. He put his hand up to his mouth to hide the smile.

Checking his watch, he saw that there was still plenty of time. He could take in the two stores near the Halstead Boulevard branch. He strolled away from the long swaths of bursting blues and greens and the drip-dry and knife-pleated, no-press, fanned out around them in great flowers.

Outside, the evening was slowly deepening. At the corner, he took a bus toward the south side of town, and he sat at the window looking at the first lights and the neon, the early glare of the city's evening. He was thinking about how different the three stores were: Cherrydale was the newest; discreet and self-conscious —a young and stylish matron in the discreetly self-conscious new shopping center. The Halstead branch was an old spinster sister, righteous, hardworking, and unpraised; plain goods and no nonsense. And then there was Lincoln Street, his big, bustling, noisy madhouse; his favorite, his firstborn, full of life and arguments and mice and problems. It sold the finest silk brocades in the city and the cheapest junk too, because the old pensioners who stayed downtown needed curtain material for thirty-nine cents a yard; and wives of foreign ambassadors and suburbanites with apartments in town bought goods from him also. He decided to close at Halstead and then go to Lincoln Street, to Home.

He got off the bus at Sixteenth and Halstead, six blocks from the store. There were two places: Loeffler's and Hagan's. He would just look in and see what was going on. When he passed Loeffler's, he decided not to go in. It was amazing how that store had gone down since he had passed it last winter. Old man Leoffler had died. Roy had heard something about a cousin running it now but whoever it was really didn't know or care about the store. He looked in the window as he went past. What a dreary, unimaginative place it had turned into. The clerks looked bitter-mouthed, and everything was sleazy and stale. In the old days, passing such a defeated place would have lighted a small glow of triumph in him, just a glimmer, before he put it out of his mind and was ashamed. Now there was only a weary sorrow. Old man Loeffler had been a hard worker—now look.

He walked on to Hagan's and was surprised to find it dark. Strange. Perhaps they had changed their nights. He looked at his watch. Nine thirty. It was better to wait a while until his own store was just ready to lock up. If he went in now, they would have to stop what they were doing, and it would mean delay and a little resentment at having to get home late. Most of the men had families. Roy was proud of the way he treated his people.

He stopped at a little coffee place and had a sweet roll and tea. His timing was right for a nice good night to everyone and that solid door latch in his hand. He sauntered up the block to pass his big store window. It was dark. He went to the door. It was closed. Dark. He tried the door a few times. Locked. But it couldn't be. Had something happened to make them leave early? He put his face to the glass to see if anyone was there, but the store was empty, shut up.

He looked at his watch again. It was 9:55, and he realized that he might have cut the time a little thin. He always allowed a full hour for finishing up; maybe they had just gotten done very quickly. The deserted store gave him an odd feeling. He had never come to a store of his at night and found it dark. It was a little like being dead, his store dark like that. He shook his head and went to the corner to catch a bus for downtown.

He was on the bus and moving before he realized that he had done it by habit, that he should have taken a cab. He wanted to hurry back to Lincoln Street, to be safe and in rhythm with the day again. He always rode the bus between the stores, and he had done it this time too, guided without his will or choice by some automatic machinery in his brain, like a drunk or a sleepwalker. It was humiliating and a little frightening, and he felt his impatience rising to his fingers to tap out the time on the window ledge while the bus crept from stop to stop in the same automatic, will-less way.

By the time it reached Eighteenth and Lincoln, Roy was trembling with impatience, and when it finally pulled up at the Seventh Street stop, he all but hurled himself out into the street. The door closed with an obscene sound behind him, and the bus pulled away while Roy stood on the curb and looked along the length of the whole store with its big window. It was dark; the whole block was dark. All up and down the block, closed faces, dead at the eyes. The streetlights were glossing them over with a cold deathshine.

He felt something go slack inside him, some soft pouch opening to let the panic slide out. He thought stupidly: Where will I go? What will I do? The panic was almost free, its smooth, cold skin pulling past his control in a rhythmic pulse, drawn and contracted. He couldn't move, and he had to sob to catch his breath. On this street for forty years—thoughts came brokenly through the rhythmic beats of fear—and no one knows me. Where can I go now?

Only after long minutes, standing and swaying in the middle of that cemetery of night-buildings, did it dawn on him that it might have been his watch. That his watch might have been wrong. He put it to his ear and heard the usual slight whir-hum. His watch didn't tick. Its parts didn't have to endure that blow of contact between springs, splines, gears, and wheels. His watch had the constant, unstopping hum of the power of a secret piece of the sun.

He lay awake all night in the elegant and coldly furnished room, in the apartment where he stayed but did not live. He could not trust enough to surrender his consciousness to sleep. In the morning, he dressed and stayed in. He sat stiffly at his small breakfast table, centered bitterly between a blaring radio and a blaring television set. The eight-o'clock news, according to his watch, was being broadcast at 6:42, the nine-o'clock report at 7:35, the ten at 8:27.

Into the world's noon he went, his head low and held forward, his face set, and through the salesroom of the Helichron Company. His pace was not the usual one for such a store; it stirred a wind behind it and a small, wavering wake of salesmen sensing trouble. He went, without needing to be told, to the second floor and from there to the office of the manager. He burst into the office and confronted the large man working over a series of blueprints and charts with a secretary and several others. Rage was beginning to seethe over the rim of his discipline. "Promises were made!" And then he threw the watch on the desk before them all, where it buried itself among the papers. "Promises were made!"

"Uh—Mr.—"

"Look at the time. Look at what time it is!"

He saw the manager weighing approaches, as he himself had done a hundred times: to be reasonable or threatening, stern or conciliatory, and wondering which one would work. To gain a minute, the manager pushed among the papers and picked up the watch. His face showed that it was visibly and incontrovertibly off time. Roy waited, tapping his foot involuntarily, like a stutter. The manager put the watch to his ear and seemed to sense the slight, almost inaudible whisper in the smooth hum, a beat that shouldn't have been there. He listened intently, his brow furrowing. There it *was* again, softly, like the sound of a leak in a valve of the heart. He took the watch from his ear.

"The cell," he said very quietly, to be quiet and reasonable, "the cell is losing its charge." Then he allowed his voice to brighten, because the thing could be dealt with, now. "Sometimes—very rarely, but sometimes—the metal governor that we've affixed to the cell undergoes a slight oxidation, and so the watch does run down instead of stopping as it should. We'll replace the watch, of couse, and give you the new cell with no charge, and we're very sorry for the inconvenience." He hadn't been looking at Roy while he spoke. Turning to prepare himself for the return of his attention to the papers on the desk, he found himself staring into Roy's face, a face contorted with terrible grief.

"You don't understand," Roy whispered hoarsely. "Promises were made—you *promised* . . ."

"But these mistakes happen, and it's nothing that we can't——"

". . . that it would stop, stop when it was still strong, that it wouldn't run down, that it would stop *before it was too late.*" And leaving the watch in the manager's hand, the hand still slightly extended toward him, Roy turned and walked from the room; and as he did, the first wave of dizziness began to darken the day before his face, and the first stroke of pain broke into the open passageways of his flesh, beginning, beginning to beat toward the visceral places, where his life was waiting, alone and unprotected.

10   The Tyrant

ONE WALL OF THE house was covered with morning-glory vines. There were overgrown bushes and big trees around the house to keep it cool and secret. Although the same bare, hot street passed in front of it, there was none of the feeling of glaring openness that made all the newer houses farther down ugly—that made her own house ugly. Willetta had come through the gate and found herself out of the summer shimmer and shielded from the children's street games and shouting. The walk up to the old house was like a cool forest place. There was thick grass growing up between the paving stones. It was cool to her feet even through her shoes. She wished she could kick off her shoes and walk barefoot, cool and silent, on the path. She looked up. The sun came green through the trees that arched the walkway and the house. Quiet rested lightly upon the leaves, and when the breeze tilted them, the quiet flowed down.

Willetta had called before coming here on her errand, and the old lady's voice, sinking and hesitant over the phone, had set the time, but as she walked up to the house Willetta didn't see the old lady or any evidence of her presence. She was used to seeing all the signs of the people who lived in a house. The other houses on the street had backyards with swing sets and barbecue equipment and washlines and half-finished patios with garden furniture that the adults never used. On the front lawns there were bicycles and tricycles, and lawn mowers and garden tools left out because the jobs they did were never finished. Saplings had been planted in the raw fill of each small lot, but they were weak and spindly; they had to be fenced and guarded from the children. All the bushes had been beaten to death in games or fights, and the flowers had been dug up by the neighborhood dogs. Willetta hated all those dogs. She couldn't feel any of the emotion of love or loss she had once had with her own dogs. It had been reduced to work and mess—the pack of them running across the yard, digging holes, dragging trash from the neighborhood cans to litter the yard, needing shots, needing food, needing care.

She went up the walk slowly and stood before the door. She had left the kids with her neighbor, but it wasn't good to take advantage. She would have to get her errand over with and be back soon. Jimmy, the baby, was colicky and fretful with the heat, and the girls had been fighting all morning. They fought because they were bored. She had spent all summer refereeing the stupid arguments they started out of boredom. If she took them swimming or to some lesson or other, the little ones came back hot and sour. With Jimmy and little Arnie it took so long to get ready to go anywhere and so long to get there that she had no energy left to want to go, and if she made herself go for their sakes, she came back to an untidy house with the day wasted and the children no less complaining.

In their new house, in the beginning, she had thought she would keep her bedroom as her quiet place. She had planned and figured and scrimped to make that room, at least, a retreat. It wasn't gay or feminine; it was a little like this walk to the old lady's house, done in soft greens and blue-greens like a cool forest path overgrown with moss and silence.

In the beginning she had imagined herself alone in that room, reading, thinking, always in quietness, listening to the quietness, her mind clear and still. But it had never been that way. In the morning she made the bed hurriedly in the beautiful room and picked up the nightclothes and the shoes and socks and Andy's crumpled shirt and left at a half-run, summoned; and she didn't come back until it was time to take off the moss- and forest-green scatter pillows and kick off her shoes and throw down the socks and shirt and go to sleep.

Last week, when Marjorie began to complain that there was no room to pratice her ballet, Willetta had gone down to the family room and brought the sewing machine and boxes of winter clothes upstairs and put them in her bedroom. It really didn't make sense, after all, to have a green forest glade without the silence or the solitude. Lately she had been almost afraid to wish for a time when she could sit quietly in that room. It made her so resentful.

She stood at the door, hoping she wouldn't wake Mrs. Ede and that she would say the right things. She began to feel hot and uncomfortable. There was no doorbell, so she knocked gently. Almost immediately there was a sound from inside, and after awhile the door opened and a voice behind it said, "Yes?"

"I'm Willetta Corder. I called you before."

"Oh, yes," the voice said vaguely, and then the door opened wider and Willetta went in.

The old woman had once been quick and thin, but lately her body had changed, and she wasn't used to carrying the extra weight. Her face and hands were thin and her legs almost sticklike; the heaviness was all in her trunk and she stood back from it, leaning away, and the clothes pulled and bunched across her protruding middle.

"You have a lovely yard," Willetta said, having to start somewhere.

The old face smiled, moving a web of wrinkles upward. Suddenly she looked much less formidable. "Do you really think so? I used to keep a nice garden, but it's gone to weeds and it's wild now. I don't have the strength to get out and work on it as I used to."

It sounded almost apologetic. She was wearing an old cotton print dress and bedroom slippers, "work clothes," and maybe she felt ashamed for not having the work to do. They went into the parlor, sun-faded and smelling of mothballs and old age, but cool and very quiet. The quiet was so rich and deep that Willetta marveled at the luxury of it. It had none of the desperation of her stolen moments or the brief lulls between uproars that she knew. It rested in layers here; it was habitual; it abided. She began to be a little jealous of this old lady, hoarding all the stillness and peace in her leaf-shaded house while the other houses down the street starved for it, stole it by minutes from grudging children and tyrannical machines. How could such a person understand the need that had made her come here?

Mrs. Ede had seen her glancing around the room. "I don't entertain any more, and I have so few visitors. I'm afraid I seldom even get to dust this room."

"I was admiring everything," Willetta said, and let her eyes go to the newly polished silver and the gleaming, mellow wood.

"I really spend most of my time in the kitchen," Mrs. Ede whispered, hand against her mouth as if she were admitting to a small sin. "Would you like to come out with me while I fix us some tea?"

But they didn't get to the kitchen. On the way the old lady remembered something upstairs, and Willetta had to go up and be shown through the rooms, Mrs. Ede stopping to point out various things that had meaning for her. They went from room to room, each perfectly kept, faded and serene. And the pictures. "That was my husband"—and she introduced Willetta to a rather vacuous, faded face on the wall. "He'll be gone eight years this February. . . . There are the girls, Alice and Susan. They're grandmothers now . . . Alice's husband passed away last fall. Those are the boys, Ronald and Richard. That was Luther, our youngest. He was killed in the war—the Second World War. . . . My grandmother gave me this blanket chest when I was married. She told me . . ."

From room to room, to the death of a son and no change of tone between that and the random, pointless facts for which the old lady seemed to want some vague enthusiasm from Willetta. Her hands caressed and picked up and straightened the old things as she passed by. When they finally went downstairs, she insisted on taking Willetta out to the back garden, where she described everything that had once been there and was there no more. In the repetitious and tiresome monologue Willetta found herself hearing a note of complacent triumph. Boys and dogs had once scoured this lovely place too. Fights and mischief had once sent a young woman running here from the hot kitchen, to save and comfort and arbitrate while the food boiled over and crusted on the stove.

". . . he put his foot right through the glass on both sides. Oh, his father was so angry. . . ." She had outlived the boys' mischief and the father's anger, the smudged walls, the endless nagging and crowding and picking up. Now instead of a trash-filled, packed-

earth backyard, trying for its small amenity with a
broken rosebush and bruised sapling there was time
for this lovely, overgrown and verdant place whose
flowers, gone wild, had spilled over their banks
and seeded among the grass and weeds, whose great
trees offered shade and quiet where a person could sit
deep in the green sunshine and eat an apple and listen.
I don't want peace at that price, Willetta thought, to
outlive it all for the sake of a little peace! But the
envy would not be shouted down. It lay undigested
in her and she felt ugly because of it.

She hinted, "My goodness, look what time it is!"
and glanced at her watch. An hour had gone by and
she hadn't even begun to explain to the old lady why
she had come. Mrs. Ede looked at her with the barest
suggestion of chiding. "Surely you have time for a little
tea. I haven't even got our tea yet!" She let Willetta
walk ahead of her up the back steps and into the old
kitchen. "Now, you just go and sit down in the
parlor," she said cheerfully, "and I'll have the tea up
in a minute." She showed Willetta back to the room in
which they had stood so briefly an hour before and
went back to the kitchen.

Mrs. Ede made sure that the sound of her work
reached the visitor. People like to know that efforts
are being made for them, she thought, that some one
is doing something. She wondered what the young woman wanted. No one ever called any more unless he
wanted something. In her day people had paid calls. She
remembered with great clarity how all the young mothers dressed their children in clean, scratchy clothes and
went calling. She saw into what seemed like hundreds
of parlors where tea things vibrated in trembling hands
with a sound as brittle as the old people's bones. It
was the old that one called on. Old Mrs. Duncan,
old Mrs. Hale. One dropped in on friends, one visited
relatives, but one called on old people. No one did

that any more. Now there was nothing to mark the days, not even a sound, and people came only to tell her what they wanted and then went away. She thought she would take a tray out and have tea in the silver service that had been a fiftieth-anniversary gift. The children had presented the sumptuous and beautiful tea set and then they had gone away, removing all the reasons for using it. She polished the pieces every week to pass the time.

As she got things ready, she realized that it was going to be difficult to serve the woman sitting in her parlor. Having many things to do and many people to consider made that woman's movements sure and lithe. Mrs. Ede spilled the sugar as she was filling the silver bowl. It was hard for her to remember how she too had once been able to move swiftly and deftly in a thousand kinds of work. What had happened to that quickness?

The water was boiling on the stove. She poured some of it into the teapot, scalding herself slightly with the steam. I raised five children, she thought, but I don't remember how. In the summer I did the wash outside. I put up pickles and preserves, I sewed. . . . But she felt it must be a lie; someone else had done all those things. How could it have been she? Hadn't she always been living alone? Tears formed in her eyes. She brushed them away quickly. What would that woman think to see her crying like a baby? She listened. The house was utterly still.

When everything was ready she took the heavy tray into the parlor, carrying it clumsily because of her bloated belly. The visitor sprang up to help, and in her embarrassment Mrs. Ede tripped over a chair leg and nearly upset the tray. Then they both murmured and soothed and apologized, making comforting mother sounds to each other. When she was settled, she poured the tea, and they went ahead with their courtesies like Japanese court women, sighing and sipping and remarking about the weather and the refreshing properties of the tea.

Neither of them wanted to begin, but at last Willetta, desperate because the afternoon was slipping away and there was a wash to get out and the ironing to start and dinner to think about, began: "Mrs. Ede, I'm here to ask, what do you intend to do with the land you have behind this street, the land in back of our lots?"

The question seemed like an insult and a trap and she couldn't think of anything to do but to say something else quickly to try to soften the question—to give a reason.

"If another developer comes in, we'll be living in a sea of houses. Our houses are built on such small lots as it is. But there's always been the relief of being able to look out the kitchen window in back and see something other than a neighbor's backyard and *her* kitchen window."

Willetta was afraid to say that some of the other women had asked her to speak for them too. She didn't want Mrs. Ede to feel that they were ganging up on her. She didn't want to seem to speak for herself alone either, because the old lady might not listen. If only she could tell, could show, how important it was, this last small vestige of daily comfort and beauty that was at stake here, waiting for a yes or no! She was a screened and shielded old lady who had quiet moments flowing from one another so steadily that she probably didn't even know how special they were to Willetta and the other women on the street, how schemed for, how pulled one by one from the resisting wheel of the day. That kitchen window was a grace used only in the moment of passing between the steps that went to pick up or put down all the food, toys, children, dog water, wash water, dust, and clothes.

The moment's glance was all she had of a distant view of anything. Her house's walls were the world now, and if someone built houses across the way, her windows would become only mirrors reflecting into infinity herself, her walls, and the small tyrannies that kept her prisoner.

"I suppose I'm here to beg you not to sell that land," she said quietly.

Mrs. Ede sat holding her teacup and wondering what to say. How very strange the world was! She had sold the first strip of land to the developers less for the money than for the people that were to come to it. She saw safety and companionship in the little community the developers had promised her would spring up around her. She had endured months of dust and mud and noise, paving and blasting and drilling and building, and endless processions of rumbling trucks and equipment so that the houses would be built and the people would come at last. When the first families moved into the miraculously wired and convenient and shining new houses on the street, she had dressed up and gone to see them. They had been busy and harried, and puzzled by her coming. They were afraid she was a busybody or an eccentric, or that she would ask them for something. She thought she might look like an old witch to them. One or two of the children had asked if she was a witch. She had tried to be pleasant. She told her new neighbors to drop by when they were settled, and to let her know if there was anything they needed. They said yes, vaguely, politely and uncomfortably, and never called. Now here was this young woman begging (yes, she had said begging) her not to let there be more houses. The development men had been around about those other eight acres, of course. She'd put them off partly because she was afraid of being cheated and partly because it kept them coming back. She had felt clumsy and stupid in the lawyer's office that first time too, pretending she understood what they were talking about when they gave her the papers to sign, and so this time she hadn't really wanted to make a decision.

"Well," she said, "I don't know," and she began to pour some more tea and offer some more of the stale cookies she had found to serve with it. Maybe she wouldn't have to decide. People take advantage of the old.

"I really am ashamed about these cookies," she said, hoping to divert the young woman, and smiled slightly with relief. In a moment or two she might get away without answering altogether. "When there is only one to cook for, you don't really cook or bake anything. When I remember all the cookies and cakes—we always used to have something to put out in case someone dropped in. I was really praised for the preserves I made. I had an apricot . . ."

Her voice drifted away. The escape she had so eagerly taken had led her only to another wall. How could that young woman believe that she had once been competent and strong? She was acting like an old woman, being tiresome and bragging about apricot preserves that couldn't mean anything to someone who had never tasted them, who could only sit patiently and listen to a stupid description of how they had once tasted in the mouths of strangers, most of whom were now dead. "I did . . . I was . . . I had . . ." All in the past, all forgotten, all meaningless. Then suddenly there was a light.

"I know what I'm going to do." She put down her cup and put her hands together in a gesture that reminded Willetta of a child praying impulsively for a new doll. "I'm going to *make* you some of my apricot preserves. Oh, it's too late for them this season, but next year. Yes, that's what I'll do!" She laughed at herself tolerantly. "It's no good telling people how good a thing is if they can't taste it, is it? I wonder how much of it I ought to make. . . ."

Please, Willetta thought, please. She wanted to read her wish into the old lady's head. I don't want your preserves or your plans or the responsibility of you. I haven't time to write another thank-you note or reciprocate with another gift or stop by or call. I don't want you on my conscience if I don't drop in. Good God, you think you want to be my mother, but you really want to be my child, and I have four children of my own and a mother who becomes a child herself if I don't phone or write every week and remember all her important dates. I have a tired husband and a lawn and a dog. Please, no more. I don't want any more! Maybe when the kids are grown enough, maybe then . . . She realized that the old lady would be gone by that time. I can't help you, she thought. I'm sorry, but I can't. Please, please don't ask me.

And so they sat still. Willetta, younger and more desperate and more resilient, came back first. "It's so beautiful here—all these big trees around the house. They keep out the glare and the dust and the noise and the feeling that you're in your neighbor's yard. But, Mrs. Ede, the newer houses don't have any trees. Everything was leveled first and the ground is still raw. It will be *years* before it is covered again, before there is any green thing to look at."

"You mustn't be discouraged," the old lady said. "Everything takes time. Before you know it those little scrubby trees will be up over your heads, and you'll have so many vines and flowers you won't know what to do with them all."

What a stupid thing to say, she thought; there are never too many flowers, there are just too few friends. How clear her memory was working in her garden and picking flowers to take whenever she went visiting! The friends were dead now and the garden was lost to weeds.

"It's wonderful to be strong," she murmured, "to be young and strong and have children growing up around you. Do you have any children, Mrs. . . ."

"Four," Willetta said. "Two boys and two girls."

"Do you sing them lullabies?" Mrs. Ede asked.

Willetta felt put off and defensive, and she was about to answer that she didn't have time for lullabies, but she realized that what she really meant was that she didn't have the tranquility, the sense of peace, that would let her unfold the night over her children loving-ly, with caresses and songs and stories. "They're all young," she said.

"Sing them lullabies," Mrs. Ede said slowly and gravely, and nodded her head. "By the time you have time they'll be gone, and when you're ready to sing to your grandchildren, your voice will be old and ugly and they won't want to kiss you when you go to visit." She looked at Willetta with a sudden piercing con-centration. "I'm not happy, Mrs. . . . I nap, but I don't sleep. I eat, but I'm never hungry any more. Do you want to know when I was happy?" Her voice had risen. "I was happy when I had to look after my hus-band and children, and when I was moving stones for my rock garden, and when I had to wash and wax the floors. I was happy when I put up my apricot pre-serves!"

The old lady's vehemence was suddenly spent, and Willetta spoke again.

"But until the trees grow, until we can have some hedges and vines, please, please don't sell that land." She glanced down at her watch. The afternoon was gone, wasted. There were baths to give, there was sup-per to fix, the wash to get out and the ironing after that, and the awful mess to clean away so they could all begin again tomorrow. She had a moment of rage, facing the old lady in her tranquil house. Mrs. Ede sat staring ahead.

"Ive been thinking of selling, but it might be a good idea to talk it over with the neighbors and see what they think. I'm sure we should all talk more about this. Why don't you drop in again next week—Tuesday afternoon, perhaps—and we can talk some more, and if the other neighbors feel as you do, perhaps the other women will come also, one or two at a time so I can get to know them. . . ."

They said good-bye, thank you, yes, lovely, working toward the door, Willetta slowly and ruthlessly pulling and Mrs. Ede slowly and ruthlessly keeping her, holding her with a sentence, and another and another, until finally Willetta managed her release. She walked down the cool front walk and out onto the hot, ugly street, striking her heels angrily. Another endless, hopeless toil. The old tyrant would demand her tribute in the scarcest commodity there was—time. Afternoons would be bound over in servitude to pay for that begrudged small freedom of the view out a kitchen window. And when the neighbors got tired of minding her children, she would be washing and dressing them to go with her, complaining, threatened into good behavior, into the old lady's fragile house. Damn you, no! she thought. You can brick up the window, but you can't make me come. My house is overpriced and I work too hard and I never have one hour to myself alone, but that old lady is overpriced too, and so is her view. There are packing boxes in my green bedroom. The world is all noise and spilled food, and to want the beauty of a window is treasonous.

Mrs. Ede gathered up the tea things and took them to the kitchen. She was excited about having the neighbor women in. It would be fun to bake with people calling and stopping by again. It was sad to have to *make* them come, but isn't it the duty of the old to teach the young? Soon they might even bring their little ones. She would try to be patient with the little ones too, and she would have to remember to get the delicate china and breakable pieces out of the way. There was no happier thing than having young people around one. When a woman's children were small, there were the other mothers to talk to, and later there was her garden club and the family, but the family was gone now, and the children and grandchildren came dutifully only during the Christmas season; they wrote or phoned only when she reminded them. She was eager to belong to these young women in their sunny, active, loud houses. How happy they were!

11   Orpheus an' Eurydice

ONE TIME THERE WAS A MAN named Orpheus, an'
the best an' only thing he liked was to play music.
Name any tune, he knew it—pick on the banjo, strum
the guitar, mouth on the trumpet, hand on the drum.
He could take up a song so strong that everybody
in sound of it couldn't help but follow, find the foot
goin', head waggin', finger snappin', took with that
tune-beat like it was come by in the blood.

He married a girl from Chickasaw. Eurydice was
her name. The music in that courtin' is spoke of yet,
how he would set out on the porch sweetenin' the
dark with sound. The animals would all go still, the
wind would lay limp in the grass so's not to blow
away one note of that sweet music. Saturday nights
he'd just empty the saloons an' pour the parties right
out folks' front doors, just so they could stand by,
quiet an' secret in the dark an' listen. Some say he
could make the stars bend to catch the sound and the
moon tip its ear.

An' they married that fall. They took their weddin'
trip to Severn Mountain. I lived on High Severn then,

an' I tell you when those two went back down-mountain, the late berries bittered up an' the wine that year tasted like wormwood. There wasn't a smile out of anyone that whole year after. None of us knew how much we could lack in the world until we had it awhile an' then lost it. Orpheus, he took up playin' for a livin'. They lived in Chilion's Grove by Kinmount an' he played weddin's, buryin's, dances, Christmas parties, for churches, saloons, and hayrides.

One spring night he come back from the Grove, from playin' a weddin', and she told him, "Orpheus, you better go for the doctor; I'm took bad." He went, but when he come back it wasn't no use. She was lyin' there, that pretty woman of his, too quiet for breathin'.

They had a big buryin'. Had a band too—all his friends. Trumpet come all the way from Franklin. They played on the way to the buryin' ground, and they was fixin' to play the way back, but Orpheus stops 'em. "That ain't *sorrow*," he says. "I want you to play sorrow, an' play it till it breaks the pain in me, a sound that'll blow through me like I was bare bone an' had no flesh to stand between me an' the sound. I want music fit to dress my grief in."

They was shamed, so they stepped back, an' then Orpheus picked up a trombone that was layin' by, an' he started playin', the sound come dark out of that horn-mouth, as dark as death an' keen-edge as death's knife. Soon the kin are cryin', an' soon the preacher is moanin', an' soon everyone is fallin' down like they was sunstruck, an' soon they got to crawl away from the sound of Orpheus playin' or the sound of grief would kill 'em sure.

Orpheus set on a gravestone by himself, playin' that trombone. It got louder, sharp as torment; louder still an' the birds fall down dead out of the sky, sea-tides stop, mountains groan to the root, leaves die on the trees, die shakin', though there ain't no wind.

Pretty soon God says, "What's cryin' out of Kinmount? The leaves an' birds are dyin' of it, the stars are commencin' to rattle in My sky."

He bends out of Halleluia an' hears the sound of Orpheus' grief risin' up, an' His soul is bit, hard bit by that sorrowin' sound.

"I never figured them war-makin' sinners could feel so deep. Sufferin' like that is too much for the small-flesh."

So He came down aside of Orpheus, an' say, "I been hearin' you play."

Orpheus says, "What's that to You? A man got a right to sound his sorrow."

God says, "You fixin' to kill everything hereabouts? I'll tell you what: I'll fix it so's you can have your woman back, only quit that trombone, or you'll freeze the sun!"

Orpheus says, "You'll give me back my wife? No joke?"

God says, "Come on an' see."

God just knocked on one of the gravestones, that's what He did. A hole opens up like an express-train light in the night, way down, farther than a man can see.

Orpheus feels the death-cold hangin' to him. They sink down into the dark—the only light was God's—down an' down.

God calls. "Eurydice, your man's come for you."

They wait. Without God there, they would have froze an' been dark-blinded. Then a white flappin' thing like an empty sheet comes quick, an' there's Eurydice standin' like a white shadow between them an' the dead that lie all down below.

"Now, mind," God says to them. "You can both go on home, but don't lay eyes on each other till you're standin' on ground. You do like I say or the deal's off an' she got to go back. Hear?"

He gives them a start an' they go on up floatin' real slow.

In a little bit, Eurydice starts complainin' "I reckon I'm changed, bein' dead an' all. The damp down there don't suit a woman's looks none."

Orpheus, he don't say nothin'.

"I been workin' it over in my mind," she says. "Is my hair gray, or maybe did I get wrinkled up from lyin' in the ground? You reckon my hair is gonna be gray when we get up home?"

He says he don't know.

It gets lighter an' she starts gettin' that kind of high voice women do when they're ready to start cryin'. "You scared to see me, Orpheus—you scared I'm gonna be ugly on account of I was dead!" An' then she busts out cryin' for real.

Man with a trained ear, he don't like listenin' to no caterwaulin'; he tells her nice to shut up, but she ain't about to quit.

"What in the Jesus-Mary do you want me to do?" he says.

She's snufflin' like a dog in a rathole. "I got to see myself. I got to know if you think I'm pretty after bein' dead like I was."

Orpheus couldn't do nothin' but suck his lip, thinkin' they was almost out of the dead-place, an' maybe he could sneak a little look just to satisfy Eurydice an' shut her up. He turned; he looked. . . .

Ain't a man livin' or dead ever hear thunder or lightnin' stitch up the sky like that. Down that dead-road the fire-branch shot light. They looked down—down a hundred miles into the secret places, death's places—an' Eurydice follows after the white-forkit branch down, down like a puff of smoke into the dark hole. He hears her give a little sob all the way down, an' the sound is all that comes risin', a little sound he can't catch hold of, an' soon the sound fades away too an' then there's nothin'. The hole is closed like it wasn't never wide as a house, an' there's Orpheus up on top of the ground right by the graves. He sets down on a gravestone an' says, "She's gone now. There ain't no comin' back from that place."

In a bit God comes, says, "Well, Orpheus——"

Orpheus stood up straight an' didn't turn away. "Maybe she was a mite vain, but she had call to be. She was a pretty woman."

God shelfed out His lip. "Well, you got her in the prettiest time. After this it's mostly downhill with women. She was twenty-two, wasn't she?"

Orpheus acted like he was readin' the ground. "Well, anyway, I'm sure gonna miss her."

"Well," says God, "lovin' adds to a man . . . but say, Orpheus, you reckon you could show me how you finger an' hitch the slide on that trombone like that? You got the best touch with it I ever did hear."

Orpheus, he just smiled a little, an' he said, "The only reason we play so good is cause we're men. We live an' die an' lose what we love. I could teach You the notes—the breathin', an' the tonguein', an' how I do with the slide—but it wouldn' sound the same."

God smiled, but it didn't fool no one. It had a sad look to it. "It's a mighty strong small-flesh I made."

Orpheus said, "Well, he ain't winter-proof, an' that's for sure. He don't last but a little. While he lasts, though, he got a powerful back for sorrow." An' he set down on a gravestone an' played for a while till God cried.

12   Upon the Waters

*To Mr. Stan Laurel and Mr. Oliver
Hardy of affectionate memory*

IT WAS A BRIGHT GREEN DAY. Big trees on the side
streets were raining seeds and the wind stirred in its
second sleep. A long flatbed truck came rattling down
one of the streets and stopped by the new steel,
chrome, and glass building. The building's lines were
so "functional" it made Cephas wonder if anyone
actually worked in it. Then he saw some women going in. Good.

He checked his appearance by hitching up to the
rearview mirror. He was wearing a clean white shirt
and a bow tie and his thin gray hair had been slicked
down with water. When he was sure he was presenta-
ble, he got down out of the cab of the truck, dusted
himself off, and began to walk slowly toward the building.

It had been many years . . . perhaps they had
moved. No, there was the sign: BOONE COUNTY
DEPARTMENT OF PUBLIC WELFARE. The last time
he had been here the building had been a temporary
shed and people had been lined up outside waiting
for the relief trucks to come. That had been in 1934,

in the winter. His father had been proud of holding out until '34.

Cephas stopped and looked at the building again. Some secretaries came out, laughing and talking. They didn't look at him, being used to seeing people who came hesitantly to their offices to acknowledge failure in life.

Cephas checked himself again in the big glass door and then went in. There was a large booth with a woman behind it and eight or nine rows of benches facing it. People were sitting quietly, staring at nothing, waiting. To the right there was a series of chutes with numbers over them. Cephas went up to the booth.

"Take a number," the woman said without looking at him.

"Ma'am?"

"You take a number and wait your turn. We'll call you."

He took one of the plastic number cards. It said 15. He sat down and waited.

"Five," the woman called. A heavy woman got up slowly and went to the booth and then to one of the chutes.

Cephas waited. Minutes were born, ripened, aged, and died without issue.

"Number six." Around him the springtime asthmatics whistled and gasped in their season. He looked at the cracks in his fingers.

"Number seven." An hour went by; another. He was afraid to go out and check his truck lest the line speed up and he lose his place.

"Number thirteen," the woman called. ...

They came to his number at last and he went up to the desk, gave back the plastic card, and was directed to his chute. Another woman was there at another desk. She took his name, Cephas Ribble, and his age, sixty-eight.

Had he been given aid before?

Yes.

Had he been on General Assistance, Aid to the Needy, Disabled or Tuberculosis Aid?

"It was what they called Relief."

"But under what category was it?"

"It was for people that was off their farms or else didn't have nothin' to eat. They called it 'goin' on the county.' It was back in nineteen and thirty-four. We held out 'till thirty-four."

"I see. . . . Now you are applying for the old-age pension?"

He said he wasn't.

"Are you married, Mr. Ribble?" She sighed.

"Never had the pleasure," he said.

"Are you without funds, in emergency status?"

He said he wasn't.

"Then take this card and go to Room Eleven, to your left." She pressed a little light or something and he felt the people shifting their weight behind him, Number 16, he supposed. He made his way to Room Eleven.

The lady there was nice; he could see it right off. She told him about the different requirement for what they called "Aid," and then she had him sign some forms: permission to inquire into his bank account, acceptance of surplus or donated food, release of medical information, and several others. Then she said sympathetically, "In what way are you disabled?"

He thought about all the ways a man might be disabled and checked each one off. It was a proud moment, a man sixty-eight without one thing in the world to complain of in his health.

"I ain't disabled no way. I am pleased you asked me, though. A man don't take time to be grateful for things like his health. If the shoe don't pinch, you don't take notice, do you?" He sat back, contented. Then he realized that the sun was getting hotter, and what with everything in the truck, he'd better get on.

The woman had put down her ball-point pen. "Mr. Ribble, if you aren't disabled or without funds, what kind of aid do you want?" A shadow of irritation crossed her face.

"No aid at all," he said. "It's about somethin' different." He tried to hold down his excitement. This was his special day, a day for which he had waited for over a decade, but it was no use bragging and playing the boy, so he said no more.

The woman was very annoyed. "Then why didn't you tell the worker at the desk?"

"She didn't give me no chance, ma'am, an' neither did that other lady. I bet you don't have many repair men comin' in here to fix things—not above once, anyway except them gets paid by the hour."

"Well, Mr. Ribble, what is it you want?" She heard the noise of co-workers leaving or returning on their coffee breaks. She sighed and began to drum her fingers, but Cephas wasn't aware of her impatience. He was beginning back in 1934. Good God, she thought, he's senile. She knew that she would have to listen to all of it. In his time, in his way.

" 'Thirty-four cleaned us out—cleaned us bare. You wonder how *farmers* could go hungry. I don't know, but we did. After the drought hit, there was nothin' to do but come in town an' sign up on the County. Twice a month my pa would come in an' bring back food. Sometimes I came with him. I seen them lines of hungry men just standin' out there like they was pole-axed an' hadn't fallen yet. I tell you, them days was pitiful, *pitiful*." He glanced at her and then smiled. "I'm glad to see *you* done good since—a new buildin' an' all. Yes, you come right up." He looked around with approval at the progress they had made.

"Mr. Ribble . . . ?"

He returned. "See, we taken the Relief, but we never got to tell nobody the good it done for us. After that year, things got a little better, and soon we was on toward bein' a payin' farm again. In 'forty-six we built us a new house—every convenience—an' in 'fifty-two we got some of them automated units for cattle care. Two years ago we dug out of debt, an' last year, I knew it was time to think about my plan for real. It was time to thank the Welfare."

"Mr. Ribble, thanks are not necessary——"

"Don't you mind, ma'am, you just get your men an' come with me."

"I beg your pardon. . . ."

"I don't just talk, ma'am; I act. You just bring your men."

Mr. Morrissey had come back from his coffee break and was standing in the hall.

The woman signaled him with her eyes as she followed Cephas Ribble, now walking proud and sure out the door to his truck. Mr. Morrissey sighed and followed, wondering why he was always around when somebody needed to make a madness plain. Why did it never happen to McFarland?

Cephas reached into his pocket and both of the welfare people thought: *Gun.* He took out a piece of paper and turned to them as they stood transfixed and pale, thinking of death. "I got it all here, all of what's in the truck. Get your men, ma'am, no use wastin' time. It's all in the truck and if it don't get unloaded soon, it's gonna spoil."

"What is this *about,* Mr. Ribble?"

"My gift, ma'am; my donation. I'm giving the Relief four hundred chickens, thirty barrels of tomatoes, thirty barrels of apricots—I figured, for variety. Don't you think the apricots was a good idea—ten barrels Eyetalian beans, six firkins of butter. . . . Ma'am, you better get the chickens out—it don't do to keep 'em in the sun. I thought about milk, so I give two cans—that's a hundred gallons of milk in case there's hungry babies."

They were dumbfounded. Cephas could see that. He wanted to tell them that it wasn't a case of trying to be big. He'd figured that everybody gave when they could. He'd even signed a form right there in the office about promising to accept donated food and clothing. Their amazement at his gift embarrassed him. Then he realized that it was probably the only way they could thank him—by making a fuss. People on the State payroll must have to walk a pretty narrow line. They'd have to be on the lookout for people taking advantage. That was it. It was deep work, that Welfare—mighty deep work.

"What are we supposed to do with all that food?" Mr. Morrissey asked.

Cephas knew that the man was just making sure that it wasn't a bribe. "Why, give it to the poor. Call 'em in an let 'em get it. You can have your men unload it right now, an' I'd do it quick if I was you. Like I said, It won't be long 'till it starts to turn in all this heat."

Mr. Morrissey tried to explain that modern welfare methods were different than those in 1934. Even then, the food had been U.S. surplus, not privately donated. It had come from government warehouses.

Cephas spoke of the stupidity and waste of Government in Farming, and rained invective on the Soil Bank.

Mr. Morrissey tried again to make his point. "We don't *give* out any food. There hasn't been any food *donated* since nineteen sixteen!"

No doubt of it, these Welfare people had to be awful careful. Cephas nodded. "The others do what they can—don't blame 'em if it don't seem like much," he said sympathetically. "I signed that slip in there about the donated food, so there must *be* a lot of donated food."

"It's an old law," Morrissey argued tiredly. "It's one of the old Poor Laws that never got taken off the books."

" 'An here you folks are followin' it, right today," Cephas mused. "It must make you mighty proud."

"Mr. Ribble, *we have no place to store all this!*"

Cephas found his throat tightening with happiness. He had come in humility, waited all morning just so he could show his small gratitude and be gone, and everyone was thunderstruck at the plenty. "Mister," he said, "I pay my taxes without complainin', but I never knowed how hard you people was workin' for your money. You got to guard against every kind of bribes an' invitations to break the law; you got to find ways to get this food to the poor people so fast, you can't even store it! By God, Mister, you make me proud to be an American!"

A policeman had stopped by the truck and was tranquilly writing a ticket. Cephas excused himself modestly and strode off to defend his situation. The two Welfare workers stood staring after him as he engaged the officers.

It was, after all, State law that food could be donated. Were there no loading ramps, no men attending them? Had the department no parking place for donors? The policeman began to look at the two stunned bearers of the State's trust. He had stopped writing.

"Could that truck fit in the workers' parking lot?" Morrissey murmured.

"What are we going to *do* with it all?" Mrs. Traphagen whimpered.

"All those chickens—four hundred chickens!"

Mrs. Traphagen sighed. "The poor will never stand for it."

"First things first," Mr. Morrissey decided, and he went to confront the policeman.

Cephas' truck in the workers' parking lot blocked all their cars. As a consequence, the aid applications of eight families were held pending investigation. Six discharged inmates of the State hospital remained incarcerated for a week longer pending home checkups. Thirty-seven women washed floors and children's faces in the expectation of home visits which did not come about. A Veneral Disease meeting at the Midtown Hotel was one speaker short, and high-school students who had been scheduled to hear a lecture entitled "Social Work, Career of Tomorrow," remained unedified. Applicants who came to apply for aid that afternoon were turned away. There was no trade in little plastic cards and the hive of offices were empty. But the people of the Boone County Department of Public Welfare were not idle. It was only that the action had moved from the desks and files and chutes to the workers' parking lot and into the hands of its glad tyrant, Cephas Ribble.

All afternoon Cephas lifted huge baskets of apricots and tomatoes into the arms of the Welfare workers. All afternoon they went from his truck to their cars, carrying baskets, or with chickens festooned limply over their arms. When they complained to Mr. Unger, the head of the department, he waved them off. Were they to go to every home and deliver the food? He said he didn't care—they were to get rid of it. Were big families to get the same amount as small families? He said that the stuff was political dynamite and that all he wanted was to be rid of it before anybody noticed.

Cephas, from the back of his flat-bed, was a titan. He lifted, smiling and loaded with a strong hand. He never stopped to rest or take a drink. The truck steamed in the hot spring light, but he was living at height, unbothered by the heat, or the closeness, or the increasing rankness of his chickens. Of course he saw that the Welfare people weren't dressed for loading food. They were dressed for church, looked like. It was deep work, very deep, working for the State. You had to set a good example. You had to dress up and talk very educated so as to give the poor a moral uplift. You had to be honest. A poor man could lie; Cephas been poor himself, so he knew; but it must be a torment to deal with people free to lie and not be able to do it yourself.

By three thirty the truck had been unloaded and Cephas was free to go home and take up his daily life again. He shook hands with the director and the case-work supervisor, the head bookkeeper and the statistician. To them he presented his itemized list, with weights carefully noted and items given the market value as of yesterday, in case they needed it for their records. Then he carefully turned the truck out of the parking lot, waved good-bye to the sweating group, nosed into the sluggish mass of afternoon traffic, and began to head home.

A cacophony of high-pitched voices erupted in the lot behind him:

"I've got three mothers of drop-outs to visit!"

"What am I going to *do* with all this stuff?"

"Who do we give this to? . . . My people won't take the Lady Bountiful bit!"

"Does it count on their food allowance? Do we go

down Vandalia and hand out apricots to every kid we see?"

"I don't have the time!"

"Which families get it?"

"Do we take the value off next month's check?"

"It's hopeless to try to distribute this fairly," the supervisor said.

"It will cost us close to a thousand dollars to distribute it at all," the statistician said.

"It would cost us close to two thousand dollars to alter next month's checks," the bookkeeper said, "and the law specifies that we have to take extra income-in-kind off the monthly allowance."

"If I were you," the director said, "I would take all this home and eat it, and not let anyone know about it."

"Mr. Morrissey!" Mrs. Traphagen's face paled away the red of her exertion, "that is fraud! You know as well as I do what would happen if it got out that we had diverted Welfare Commodites to our own use! Can you imagine what the Mayor would say? The Governor? The State Department of Health? The HEW, The National Association of Social Workers?!" She had begun to tremble and the two chickens that were hanging limply over her arm nodded to each other with slow decorum, their eyes closed righteously against the thought.

Cars began to clot the exit of the parking lot. The air was redolent.

But many of the workers didn't take the food home. The wolf of hunger was patient in shadowing the poor, even in summer, even on Welfare. As the afternoon wore on, apricots began to appear in the hands of children from Sixteenth and Vandalia Street all the way to the Boulevard. Tomatoes flamed briefly on the windowsills of the Negro ghetto between Fourteenth and Kirk, and on one block, there was a chicken in every pot.

The complaints began early the next day. Sixteen Negroes called the Mayor's Committee on Racial Harmony, claiming that chickens, fruit, and vegetables had been given to the White Disadvantaged, while they had received tomatoes, half of them rotten. A rumor began that the food had been impregnated with contraceptive medicine to test on the poor and that three people had died from it. The Health Department denied this, but its word was not believed.

There were eighteen calls at the Department of Welfare protesting a tomato fight which had taken place on Fourteenth and Vandalia, in which passers-by had been pelted with tomatoes. The callers demanded that the families of those involved be stricken from the Welfare rolls as Relief cheaters, encouraging waste and damaging the moral fiber of working people.

Eighteen mothers on the Aid to Dependent Children program picketed the Governor's mansion, carrying placards that read: *Hope, Not Handouts* and *Jobs, Not Charity.*

Sixty-eight welfare clients called to say that they had received no food at all and demanded equal service. When they heard that the Vandalia Street mothers were picketing, a group of them went down as counter-pickets. Words were exchanged between the two groups and a riot ensued in which sixteen people were hospitalized for injuries, including six members of the city's riot squad. Seven of the leaders were arrested and jailed pending investigation. The FBI was called into the case in the evening to ascertain if the riot was Communist-inspired.

At ten o'clock the Mayor appeared on TV with a plea for reason and patience. He stated that the riot was a reflection of the general decline in American morals and a lack of respect for the law. He ordered a six-man commission to be set up to hear testimony and make recommendations. A political opponent demanded a thorough investigation of the county Welfare system, the War on Poverty, and the local university's radicals.

The following day, Mrs. Traphagen was unable to go to work at the Welfare office, having been badly scalded on the hand while canning a bushel of apricots.

Cephas Ribble remembered everyone at the Welfare Office in his prayers. After work, he would think about the day he had spent in the city, and of his various triumphs: the surprise and wonder on the faces of the workers; the open awe of the lady who had said, "You don't need to thank us." How everyone had dropped the work they were doing and ran to unload the truck. It had been a wonderful day. He had given his plenty unto the poor, the plenty and nourishment of his own farm. He rose refreshed to do his work, marveling at the meaning and grandeur with which his chores were suddenly invested.

"By God," he said, as he checked the chickens and noted their need for more calcium in the feed, "a man has his good to do. I'm gonna do it every year. I'm gonna have a day for the poor. Yessir, every year." And he smiled genially on the chickens, the outbuildings, and the ripening fields of a generous land.